The Abortion Debate

ISSUES

Volume 126

Series Editor

Craig Donnellan

Assistant Editor

Lisa Firth

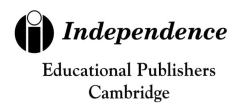

Independence

Educational Publishers
Cambridge

First published by Independence
PO Box 295
Cambridge CB1 3XP
England

British Library Cataloguing in Publication Data
The Abortion Debate – (Issues Series)
I. Donnellan, Craig II. Series
363.4'6

ISBN 1 86168 365 0

Printed in Great Britain
MWL Print Group Ltd

Layout by
Lisa Firth

Cover
The illustration on the front cover is by
Angelo Madrid.

CONTENTS

Chapter One: Abortion Facts

Chapter Two: The Debate

Introduction

The Abortion Debate is the one hundred and twenty-sixth volume in the **Issues** series. The aim of this series is to offer up-to-date information about important issues in our world.

The Abortion Debate looks at facts about abortion, as well as presenting an overview of the debate surrounding this controversial issue.

The information comes from a wide variety of sources and includes:
Government reports and statistics
Newspaper reports and features
Magazine articles and surveys
Website material
Literature from lobby groups
and charitable organisations.

It is hoped that, as you read about the many aspects of the issues explored in this book, you will critically evaluate the information presented. It is important that you decide whether you are being presented with facts or opinions. Does the writer give a biased or an unbiased report? If an opinion is being expressed, do you agree with the writer?

The Abortion Debate offers a useful starting-point for those who need convenient access to information about the many issues involved. However, it is only a starting-point. Following each article is a URL to the relevant organisation's website, which you may wish to visit for further information.

*****

Religion, contraception and abortion

Information from the fpa

fpa putting sexual health on the agenda

Introduction

This article aims to reflect the attitudes and beliefs of the leading religious groups in the United Kingdom to contraception and abortion.

The 2001 Census[1] showed that just over three-quarters of the UK population reported following a religion, and, although there is a wide range of religious groups in the UK, the seven most commonly followed faiths are represented in this article.

Religion and culture

Although the two are inextricably linked, the distinction between culture and religion needs to be recognised. Religion is a powerful influence on sexual attitudes and behaviour in many individuals and it often forms a society's orientation towards human sexuality. When a particular religion is practised by many people in a society, it helps create culture, which then influences even those that don't accept the religion.[2]

Personal interpretations of any faith may vary from the liberal to strictly traditional, depending on the individual. Influences such as ethnicity, age, sex and social class as well as culture can all have an effect on how someone views a religious faith. Religious doctrines can be viewed as a means to a spiritual goal, rather than merely a restriction on what is and is not acceptable.[3]

Throughout history religion has provided society with a great deal of information about sexuality. Many of these societies subsequently used this information to create laws regulating sex. However, it is important that these laws are seen in their historical context. Whilst a basic understanding of religious and cultural beliefs is useful, generalisations should be avoided.

Most of the following sections have been either written by or based on advice from the relevant religious groups. Where advice could not be obtained, other sources have been used.

Church of England

Contraception

Contraception is acceptable to most in the Church of England, as long as it is mutually acceptable to both partners. It is generally agreed that parents have a responsibility to decide the number and spacing of their children, decisions based on the needs of existing children, prospects for maternal and child health and the particular social context.

However, Anglican tradition allows for a wide range of views, all of which are held sincerely and reached after much thought and prayer.
Source: General Synod of the Church of England, Board for Social Responsibility. 'What is the Church's View?'

Abortion

The Church of England combines strong opposition to abortion with the recognition that there can be – strictly limited – conditions under which it may be morally preferable to any available alternative.
Source: General Synod Resolution.

Text approved by the Church of England Archbishops' Council.

Catholicism

Contraception

Responsible parenthood will often involve planning when to have children, God willing, but the Catholic Church believes that this should not be by artificial means since the Church believes such actions undermine the full meaning of human sexuality. The last 20 years have seen great improvements in natural family planning, which is now regarded as being highly effective for those who are instructed by trained teachers

and who are strongly motivated. The values of this holistic and human approach to family planning deserve to be considered seriously.
Source: Cherishing Life #125-126.

Abortion

The Catholic Church regards abortion as the termination of a human life. The law of the Church establishes that a person who actually procures an abortion, fully aware of what they are doing, incurs the penalty of excommunication that can only be rescinded through the sacrament of reconciliation. Having acknowledged the unborn child, the Church recognises the difficult circumstances that expectant mothers sometimes find themselves in and also the responsibilities of others.

Religion is a powerful influence on sexual attitudes and behaviour in many individuals and it often forms a society's orientation towards human sexuality

---

The Church wishes to protect the lives of unborn children and also to support expectant mothers so they do not feel forced to make such a harmful choice. The Church welcomes women who feel remorse over an abortion and who come seeking forgiveness, reconciliation and absolution.
Source: Cherishing Life #173-176.

Cherishing Life is a teaching document recently published by the Catholic Bishops of England and Wales.

Text approved by Department of Christian Responsibility and Citizenship, Catholic Bishops' Conference of England and Wales.

Islam

Contraception

Whilst pre-marital sex is prohibited, a sexual relationship is seen as part of married life, both for the purposes of having children and to ensure that the sexual needs of the couple are satisfied within a legitimate relationship. Contraception has been judged permissible in certain circumstances:

■ to space child-bearing, thus promoting the health of all children in the family. For example, to protect the health of an existing child who may not yet be weaned.
■ where there is fear for the physical and mental well-being of the mother.
■ for personal reasons dictated by conscience.

Coitus interruptus, the withdrawal method, was practised by early Muslims with the tacit approval of Prophet Muhammad (peace be upon him). Some Muslim jurists have inferred from this that other non-permanent methods such as condoms, cap, intra-uterine device (IUD) and oral contraceptives are also permissible.

Vasectomy is strictly forbidden. Although female sterilisation may be permissible, this is only when there is a medical opinion that the woman's life would be endangered or her mental health seriously affected by a pregnancy, which could not be prevented by other legitimate means.

Abortion

Abortion is never permitted as a means of birth control. Allah tells us in the Qur'an:

'Kill not your children for fear of want. We shall provide sustenance for them as well as for you. Verily the killing of them is a great sin.'
Source: Qur'an 17:31 YA.

Text approved by the IQRA Trust.

Sikhism

Contraception

Sikhs believe in monogamy and great importance is attached to high moral character, modesty and sexual morality. One of the five Ks (religious symbol) of Sikhs is Kachhahra, which is a special pair of shorts worn as an undergarment by all initiated Sikhs, both men and women. This highlights the importance attached to sexual morality in Sikhism. Traditionally in Sikhism, like many other religions, the family size used to be large. However, attitudes today are beginning to change. Birth control

through the use of contraception is an acceptable practice within Sikhism and family size is usually small. As there is no actual religious prohibition, acceptance of family planning has grown in line with social and cultural changes.

Abortion

Abortion is accepted only in extreme circumstances such as rape or to save the mother's life.

Text approved by the Sikh Education Council.

Hinduism

Hinduism is a way of life as well as a religion. In Hinduism, four possible approaches to life are acceptable:

■ *karma* – the pursuit of pleasure;
■ *artha* – the pursuit of power and material wealth;
■ *dharma* – the pursuit of the moral life;
■ *moksha* – the pursuit of liberation through the negation of the self.

The Hindu religion has evolved over thousands of years and is extremely diverse with a varied mythology and a complex approach to practice. However, many positive approaches to sexuality can be found in Hinduism.

Contraception

All methods of contraception are permitted.

Arguments for family planning can be found in many moral teachings and epic stories such as the *Mahabharat* which 'offers great praise for the Pandavas, who served as one of the Hindu prototypes of the ideal family. The Pandavas have small families and are exemplary in meeting the exacting demands of dharma'.[4]

Many Hindus believe that it is their duty to produce a son, since only sons can perform the funeral rites that enable a man's soul to go to heaven. Sons are therefore needed to say prayers to ensure survival in the next world. A son is known as 'putra' – he who saves from hell. Contraception is therefore not generally practised until the birth of a son or sons.

Abortion

Abortion tends to be disapproved of as Hindus believe that both physical and spiritual life enter the human embryo at the moment of conception. To Hindus all life is sacred. However, in keeping with the diversity within the Hindu faith there are varying views on the subject of abortion and there is evidence that abortion is an accepted part of modern life for many Hindus. India is a country where over 80% of the population are Hindus[5] and Hindu religious bodies hold strong views on most moral issues. Despite this, abortion was legalised in India in 1971 in cases of rape, incest and for the mental health of the woman if she would be adversely affected by the birth of an unwanted child.

Judaism

Family and community are at the core of Jewish religious practice. The basic source of the Judeo-Christian tradition is the Old Testament of the Bible, which gives a fundamentally positive view of sexuality.

Contraception

The sources in Jewish law state categorically that a man may not use any form of contraception. However, as any mention of females and contraception was omitted from the sources, most if not all use this omission to interpret that females may use contraception. For those that believe no physical impediment may be used, even for females, oral contraception may constitute an exception as the pill does not interfere in any way with the natural act of intercourse and the male seed is not directly destroyed.

Contraception can be used by a woman whose physical or psychological health is at risk by becoming pregnant.

Abortion

As a rule, abortion is prohibited unless the life of the mother is at risk, or if continuing the pregnancy causes a severe threat to her health. Although termination is not ideal there are exceptional circumstances, such as rape, where abortion is not forbidden. In these situations the rabbi would provide guidance as to the best course of action.

Buddhism

Buddhists are the arbiters of their own destiny. Cultural and other influences apart, they are free to act according to their own insights and understanding. They are, however, taught to act responsibly and to take complete responsibility for the effects of these actions. In acting thus they would be guided by certain personal undertakings. Foremost amongst these would be the undertaking to avoid intentional harm to any living (breathing) thing, cultivating as integral to this, genuine attitudes of loving kindness (*metta*) and compassion (*karuna*) with regard to them.

Source: The Buddhist Society.

Contraception

Most Buddhists believe that conception occurs when the egg is fertilised so contraception that prevents fertilisation is not ordinarily a problem. Emergency contraception is likely to be unacceptable. However, as Buddhism is open to personal interpretation, attitudes to this and other questions of birth control will vary.

Abortion

Most Buddhists believe in reincarnation and this has a direct bearing on their views on abortion. Buddhists believe that consciousness enters the womb and human life begins at the moment of conception. This suggests that the foetus has rights equal to that of an adult, therefore terminating a pregnancy could be seen as killing a sentient being. Although it is a point of ethical debate, many Buddhists do not believe all beings are equal and if continuing the pregnancy posed a severe health risk to the woman, the foetus would not be seen as equal to the woman.

References

1   Religion in Britain.
2   Hyde J S, *Understanding Human Sexuality*, 5th ed., New York: Mc-Graw-Hill, 1994).
3   Blake S and Katrak Z, *Faith, Values and Sex and Relationships Education* (London: National Children's Bureau, 2002).
4   Maguire D C, *Sacred Choices. The Right to Contraception and Abortion in Ten World Religions* (Minneapolis: Augsburg Fortress, 2001; p53).
5   *Census of India 1991*, Table C-9, Part VB(ii) – Religion.

Further reading

■ Hallgarten L, *Abortion Rights, Responsibilities and Reason* (London: Education For Choice, 2004).

■ Halstead J M and Reiss M J, *Values in Sex Education: From Principles to Practice* (London: Routledge Farmer, 2003).

■ Health Education Authority, *Sex Education, Values and Morality* (London: HEA, 1994).

■ The above information is reprinted with kind permission from the fpa. Visit www.fpa.org.uk for more information.

© fpa

A *humanist* discussion of *abortion*

Information from the British Humanist Association

Humanists seek to live good lives without religious or superstitious beliefs. They use reason, experience and respect for others when thinking about moral issues, not obedience to dogmatic rules. So in thinking about abortion a humanist would consider the evidence, the probable consequences, and the rights and wishes of everyone involved, trying to find the kindest course of action or the one that would do the least harm. Abortion is an issue that demonstrates the difficulties of rigid rules in moral decision making. Medical science has advanced to the point where we have options that were unthinkable even a few generations ago and where old rules cannot cope with new facts.

Some medical facts

- Some very premature babies can now be kept alive, which has altered ideas about when foetuses become human beings with human rights. The law in England and Wales is based on the fact that after 24 weeks the foetus is often viable, in that with medical assistance it can survive outside the womb.
- Many illnesses and disabilities can now be diagnosed long before birth.
- Some very ill or disabled babies who would probably once have died before or shortly after birth can now be kept alive.
- The sex of a foetus can be known well before birth (and some parents would like to be able to choose the sex of their child).
- Genetic research makes it increasingly likely that parents will be able to know, or even to choose, other characteristics for their unborn child. A few will want to reject some foetuses.

BRITISH HUMANIST ASSOCIATION
for the one life we have

- Abortions can be performed safely, though they can occasionally cause medical or psychological problems.

These are in themselves morally neutral medical facts, but they bring with them the necessity to make moral choices and to consider who should make those choices. Doctors? Politicians? Religious leaders? Medical ethics committees? Individual women? Their partners?

Some views on abortion

Some examples of contemporary rules and views about abortion will perhaps demonstrate the complexity of the problem.

- Some religious people think that all human life is sacred, that life begins at conception, and so abortion is always wrong (and some also believe that contraception is wrong, which leads to even more unwanted pregnancies). But a humanist would argue that the idea of 'sacredness' is unhelpful if one has to choose between risking the life of the mother or the life of the unborn foetus. (This is very rare these days, and the choice is most often about the quality of life of either the mother or the foetus or both).
- People often argue that it is not for doctors 'to play God' and that it is for God to decide matters of life and death. But it could be said that all medical interventions are 'playing God' (even your childhood vaccinations may have kept you alive longer than 'God' planned), so we have to decide for ourselves how we use medical powers. Arguments which invoke God are unconvincing to those who do not believe in gods, and laws should not be based on claims which rely on religious faith.
- Some (non-religious) moral philosophers have argued that full consciousness begins only after birth or even later, and so foetuses and infants are not full human beings with human rights.
- Doctors have a range of opinions on abortion, but tend to give the medical interests of the mother (which may include her mental health) the most weight when making decisions.

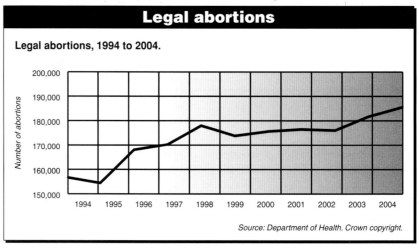

Legal abortions

Legal abortions, 1994 to 2004.

Source: Department of Health. Crown copyright.

- Some doctors and nurses dislike carrying out abortions because they feel that their job is to save life, not to destroy it.
- Some people believe that a woman has absolute rights over her own body which override those of any unborn foetus. You might like to read Judith Jarvis Thomson's *A Defense of Abortion* which states a feminist case for abortion very clearly.

The current law is permissive: it does not impose abortion on anyone who does not want one or want to perform one

---

- The law in England, Scotland and Wales permits abortion before the 24th week of pregnancy if two doctors agree that there is a risk to the life or the mental or physical health of the mother if the pregnancy continues, or there will be a risk to the mental or physical health of other children in the family. However, there is no time limit if there is a substantial risk that the baby will be born severely disabled, or there is a grave risk of death or permanent injury (mental or physical) to the mother. In effect this means that almost every woman who wants an abortion and is persistent in seeking one before the 24th week can obtain one. However, some women who do not realise that they are pregnant till too late (perhaps because they are very young or because they are menopausal) may not be able to have abortions though they would have qualified on other grounds.

The humanist view

The current law is permissive: it does not impose abortion on anyone who does not want one or want to perform one. So even within the law, individuals have to make moral choices. How do humanists pick their way between these conflicting ideas? Humanists value life and value happiness and personal choice, and many actively campaigned for legalised abortion in the 1960s. Although humanists do not think all life is 'sacred' they do respect life, and much in this debate hinges on when one thinks human life begins. Humanists tend to think that a foetus does not become a person, with its own feelings and rights, until well after conception.

Because humanists take happiness and suffering into consideration, they are usually more concerned with the quality of life than the right to life, if the two come into conflict. The probable quality of life of the baby, the woman, rights and wishes of the father and the rest of the family, and the doctors and nurses involved, would all have to be given due weight. There is plenty of room for debate about how much weight each individual should have, but most humanists would probably put the interests of the woman first, since she would have to complete the pregnancy and probably care for the baby, whose happiness would largely depend on hers. She also exists already with other responsibilities and rights and feelings that can be taken into account – unlike those of the unborn foetus which cannot be so surely ascertained.

Of course all possible options should be explored and decisions should be informed ones. Adoption of the unwanted baby might be the best solution in some cases, or on reflection a woman might decide that she could look after a sick or disabled child. Or she might decide that she cannot offer this child a life worth living and abortion is the better choice. She will need to consider the long-term effects as well as the immediate ones. It is unlikely to be an easy decision, and requiring an abortion is a situation that most women would prefer to avoid.

For society as a whole, as well as for the children themselves, it is better if every child is a wanted child. However, abortion is not the best way of avoiding unwanted children, and improved sex education, easily available contraception, and better education and opportunities for young women, can all help to reduce the number of abortions. But as long as abortion is needed as a last resort, most humanists would agree that society should provide safe legal facilities. The alternatives, which would inevitably include illegal abortions, are far worse.

Questions to think about and discuss

- Is abortion in the case of conception after rape more justified than other abortions?
- Would a humanist favour abortion if a woman wanted one because her pregnancy was interfering with her holiday plans? Why (not)?
- Why do humanists think contraception is better than abortion?
- Are there any good arguments against adoption of unwanted babies?
- Should doctors and nurses impose their moral views on patients? Yes? Sometimes? Never?
- Should religious people impose their views on abortion on non-religious people? Yes? Sometimes? Never?
- Should parents be able to choose the sex of their child? Should they be able to abort a foetus of the 'wrong' sex?
- At what point does a foetus become a human being? Does this affect the humanist view of abortion? Does this affect your view of abortion?
- Can infanticide ever be right?
- Should abortion ever be carried out on a non-consenting woman, e.g. one too young to give legal consent or one in a coma?
- How are you deciding your answers to these questions? What principles and arguments influence your answers?
- How is the humanist view on this issue similar to that of other worldviews you have come across? How is it different?

Updated January 2006

Termination

Information from the National Youth Agency

Some facts about termination (also called abortion):

- One in five pregnancies in the UK end in termination;
- 90% of all abortions take place in the first 12 weeks of pregnancies;
- More than half of all pregnancies in under 16s end in abortion.

Abortion is a sensitive issue and is in fact illegal in some cultures and countries. It is legal in the UK but on the grounds of religious belief, it is illegal in the Republic of Ireland. Anti-abortion campaigners ask the question of whether or not the foetus is alive, whether it has an individual right to life and whether the woman has the right to choose whether or not she continues with a pregnancy.

Abortion and religion

It is often people with a committed religious viewpoint who oppose abortion, although some religions are more tolerant than others when it comes to abortion when there is danger to the mother's life. Abortion is opposed on the grounds that all life is sacred and at whatever stage in its development, human life must not be destroyed. It is often based on these religious grounds that countries develop their legal position on abortion. In the Republic of Ireland for example, the Catholic majority population has opposed abortion: it is therefore illegal to have an abortion there. However, Islam teaches that life is sacred and that an abortion can only be carried out if the woman's life is in danger. In this case the mother's life takes precedence over the baby's.

Abortion and the law

In England, Scotland and Wales abortion is regulated by the Abortion Act 1967. It accepts that abortion is justified but only in certain circumstances and before the 24th week of the pregnancy. The Act says that:

The National Youth Agency

- an abortion can legally be carried out if two doctors agree that to continue the pregnancy would put the mother's life at risk or she is at risk of physical or mental injury (which can include serious emotional strain, depression and other forms of mental stress); or
- two doctors agree that the child is likely to be born with severe mental or physical disability.

An abortion must be carried out before the 24th week of pregnancy, unless a serious risk of life occurs to the mother beyond this period.

If you are under 16 either your parents must give their consent or else the two doctors who agree to the termination must also agree that you are mature enough to understand what their decision means. If the abortion is being carried out after eight weeks then it will be under a general anaesthetic, in which case permission may be required from your parents if you are under 16.

The would-be father (whether married or not) has no legal right to prevent the mother from having an abortion. The decision is hers.

The Abortion Act allows doctors and other medical staff to refuse any involvement in the practice of abortion if it is against their conscience. This means that you may want an abortion but your GP will not support you. In a situation like this you can go to another GP for medical advice (you don't have to be registered with that GP if you go for family planning or abortion advice). The GP will then contact your local hospital for an appointment with the second doctor.

Over half of all pregnancies in under 16s end in abortion

Because of the 24-week time factor in terminating a pregnancy and because the number of clinics doing abortions are limited, it is often necessary to travel some distance for an abortion.

In addition to the physical discomfort and pain of an abortion (particularly if it is carried out after 12 weeks) many women have mixed feelings of loss and relief.

Abortion is a taboo subject (one that some people do not like to talk about); it is often more difficult to talk about how you feel to friends

Abortions by age group

Legal abortions by age group,[1] 2004, England and Wales residents. Rates per 1,000 women.[2]

1. Age not stated have been distributed pro-rata across age group 20-24.
2. All rates are based on 2004 projected populations.
3. Rates for under 15 are based on populations 13-14.

Source: Department of Health. Crown copyright.

and family. It is a painful emotional experience and you may wish to contact one of the organisations below for support.

Organisations

Abortion Rights

Abortion Rights believes women should be allowed to make up their own minds on abortion, regardless of their circumstances. Women should not be forced by law to rely on the decision of their doctors, who are sometimes influenced by moral rather than medical judgement.
Telephone: 020 7923 9792
Address: 18 Ashwin Street, London, E8 3DL.
Fax: 020 7923 9792
Website: www.abortionrights.org.uk

British Pregnancy Advisory Service (BPAS)

BPAS sees many women who are faced with an unplanned pregnancy and find it hard to make a decision about what to do. It is contacted by almost 50,000 women every year.
Helpline: 08457 30 40 30

Telephone: 0870 365 5050
Fax: 0870 365 5051
Address: 4th floor, Amec House, Timothy's Bridge Road, Stratford-upon-Avon, CV37 9BF.
Website: www.bpas.org
Opening hours: BPAS Action Line open Monday-Friday 8am-9pm Saturday 8.30am-6pm and Sunday 9.30am-2.30pm.

LIFE (Save the Unborn Child)

LIFE is a campaigning group who oppose abortion, believing that every unborn child has the right to life. If you feel that LIFE may be able to help you, contact them at the address below.
Helpline: 01926 311511
Telephone: 01926 421587
Address: 1a Newbold Terrace, Leamington Spa, Warwickshire CV32 4GA.
Fax: 01926 336497
Email: info@lifeuk.org
Website: www.lifeuk.org
Opening hours: The helpline is available between 9am and 9pm daily.

NHS Direct

NHS Direct is a 24-hour nurse-led telephone advice and information service and is part of the National Health Service.
Telephone: 0845 46 47
Email: feedback@nhsdirect.nhs.uk
Website: www.nhsdirect.nhs.uk
Opening hours: open 24 hours a day, 7 days a week.

Support After Termination for Abnormality (SATFA)

SATFA provides information and support to families who are told that their unborn baby may have an abnormality. They also offer long-term support to parents who choose termination.
Telephone: 020 7439 6124
Address: 73 Charlotte Street, London W1 1LB.
Fax: 020 7631 0285

■ The above information is reprinted with kind permission from the National Youth Agency. Please visit their website at www.youthinformation.com for more information.

© National Youth Agency

The legal position

The history of British abortion law

Abortion in England and Wales was first made illegal in the 19th century. Before then English Common Law had allowed abortion provided it was carried out before the woman felt the foetus move ('quickening') when it was believed the soul entered the body.

Abortions performed after quickening were an offence under Common Law but there were no fixed penalties and the woman having the abortion was not necessarily held responsible. In 1803 the law changed and abortion became a criminal offence from the time of conception, with penalties of up to life imprisonment for both the pregnant woman and the abortionist.

The Offences against the Person Act 1861

Section 58 of the Offences against the Person Act 1861 made abortion a criminal offence punishable by imprisonment from three years to life, even when performed for medical reasons. No further legal changes occurred in England until 1929. The Offences Against the Person Act is still in place and the current law simply provides exceptions to the 1861 law by clarifying when an abortion can be legal.

The Infant Life Preservation Act 1929

The Infant Life Preservation Act amended the law so that abortion would no longer be regarded as a felony if it was carried out in good faith for the sole purpose of preserving the life of the mother.

The 1929 Act made it illegal to kill a child 'capable of being born live', and set 28 weeks as the age at which a foetus was assumed to be able to survive.

The Infant Life Preservation Act has never applied in Scotland.

The 'Bourne judgment' 1938

In 1938, Dr Alex Bourne performed an abortion on a 14-year-old girl after a gang of soldiers had raped her. Dr Bourne informed the police

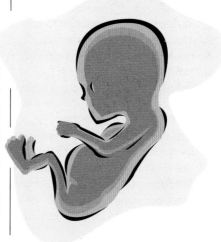

and was prosecuted. In court, the judge ruled that Dr Bourne had acted in the 'honest belief' that the abortion would 'preserve the life of the mother'.

Abortion in England and Wales was first made illegal in the 19th century. Before then English Common Law had allowed abortion

---

This opened the way for other doctors to interpret the law more flexibly because it established that preserving a woman's life could mean more than literally preventing her death.

The Abortion Act 1967

The Abortion Act 1967 came into effect on 27 April 1968 and permits termination of pregnancy subject to certain conditions. Regulations under the Act mean that abortions must be performed by a registered practitioner in a National Health Service hospital or in a location that has been specially approved by the Department of Health – such as a BPAS clinic.

An abortion may be approved providing two doctors agree in good faith that one or more of the following criteria apply:

- the continuance of the pregnancy would involve risk to the life of the pregnant woman greater than if the pregnancy were terminated;
- the termination is necessary to prevent grave permanent injury to the physical or mental health of the pregnant woman;
- the continuance of the pregnancy would involve risk, greater than if the pregnancy were terminated, of injury to the physical or mental health of the pregnant woman;
- the continuance of the pregnancy would involve risk, greater than if the pregnancy were terminated, of injury to the physical or mental health of any existing child(ren) of the family of the pregnant woman;

- there is a substantial risk that if the child were born it would suffer from such physical or mental abnormalities as to be seriously handicapped;

Or in an emergency, certified by the operating practitioner, as immediately necessary:

- to save the life of the pregnant woman; or

- to prevent grave permanent injury to the physical or mental health of the pregnant woman.

In relation to grounds 3 and 4 the doctor may take account of the pregnant woman's actual or reasonably foreseeable environment, including her social and economic circumstances.

Most abortions of unwanted pregnancies are carried out under grounds 3 or 4 because the doctor confirms that it would be damaging to the woman's mental health to force her to continue the pregnancy.

Doctors and other medical staff have the legal right to 'conscientiously object' to taking part in abortions unless this is necessary to save the life or prevent grave permanent injury to the woman.

Human Fertilisation and Embryology Act 1990

Section 37 of the Human Fertilisation and Embryology Act made changes to the Abortion Act. It introduced a time limit of 24 weeks for grounds 3 and 4. Grounds 1, 2 and 5 are now without limit. Before this change, a 28-week limit had applied for all grounds.

The Human Fertilisation and Embryology Act also confirmed that when a woman had a multiple pregnancy it was legal for a doctor to terminate the life of one or more foetuses, leaving others alive.

The Abortion Act 1967 and Section 37 of the Human Fertilisation and Embryology Act 1990 do not apply to Northern Ireland.

- The above information is reprinted with kind permission from the British Pregnancy Advisory Service. Visit www.bpas.org for more information.

© BPAS

Abortions by marital status

Legal abortions by marital status, 2004, percentage.[1] England and Wales residents.

	Percentage
Single no partner	31%
Single with partner	29%
Single not stated	17%
Single (total)	77%
Married	18%
Separated	2%
Widowed	0%
Divorced	2%

1. Percentages exclude not known and not stated.
Note: percentages are rounded and may not necessarily add to 100.

Source: Department of Health. Crown copyright.

Coping with an unplanned pregnancy

Terminating a pregnancy is a major decision and a difficult one to make. Dr Sarah Brewer outlines the options

Despite the availability of effective contraception, it is estimated that one in three babies is unplanned – though not necessarily unwanted. Many unplanned pregnancies end in abortion, which is the voluntary termination of pregnancy. If you do find yourself unexpectedly pregnant and are unsure whether you want to give birth to the baby, it's important to consider all your options carefully so as to make the right decision for you.

Your options include keeping the baby, having the baby cared for by relatives more able to take on this responsibility, having the baby adopted, or having a termination of pregnancy

Your options include keeping the baby, having the baby cared for by relatives more able to take on this responsibility than yourself, having the baby adopted through an agency, or having a termination of pregnancy. Abortion is a legal procedure and every woman's right, should she not want to go through with the pregnancy.

Termination for abnormality

Sadly, between 2 and 5 per cent of babies conceived have a congenital abnormality, which may be associated with a variety of special needs. This will usually be detected during the routine ultrasound scans and, if the abnormality is severe, you may be offered a termination

*i*Village.co.uk™
the website for women

for abnormality. When faced with having to make such a difficult decision, it may help to know that the national charity, Antenatal Results and Choices (ARC), is available to befriend and support those considering antenatal testing, those who are waiting anxiously for test results, and those who are faced with the difficult decision about whether or not to end an abnormal pregnancy.

Making the decision – weighing up options

On discovering you are pregnant, your doctor is a good first port of call. He or she can confirm how advanced the pregnancy is, provide information on the options available in your local area, and refer you for counselling.

The decision to have an abortion is not a decision you should have to make on your own, so try to bring yourself to talk to your partner and, if appropriate, family and friends, to see if there is any way you can manage to fit a baby into your life. It may be that you would feel happier having the baby and placing him or her for adoption. Only take the decision to terminate the pregnancy once you have fully considered that this is the only option for you.

If you decide a termination is the best decision for you, try to talk through your decision with supportive people. This will help you to feel more reconciled with it later. Clinics offering abortion will have supportive counsellors available for you to discuss your decision with.

You can also speak to someone at the Pregnancy Crisis and Post Abortion Careline, tel: 0800 028 2228, to help you discover more clearly how you feel about the situation you are in. The counsellors are trained in non-directional counselling – so you will not be pushed in one direction or the other.

Requesting an abortion

If you decide to have a termination, you will need to see your doctor as soon as possible. Most abortions are between the seventh and 16th week of pregnancy, ideally before the 12th week of pregnancy.

Research involving over 9,000 women has found no difference in fertility rates between those who had previously had a termination, compared with those who had not

---

Although a termination can be performed up until the 24th week of pregnancy, this is getting very close to the time when a foetus is capable of surviving on its own with appropriate intensive neonatal care. For ethical reasons, some doctors prefer not to carry out terminations at this stage, and some will not carry out the procedure if you are more than 12 weeks pregnant.

Abortion procedures

In some cases you may be offered a medical termination that does not involve surgery. You will be given a tablet called Mifepristone, which works by blocking the action of the pregnancy hormone, progesterone. After taking the Mifepristone, a vaginal pessary that softens the cervix will be inserted 36 to 48 hours later, and a 'spontaneous' miscarriage will usually follow. Medical abortion only fails once in a hundred pregnancies.

A surgical termination of pregnancy is carried out under general anaesthetic. A pessary may be inserted beforehand to help soften the cervix and make the procedure easier. The surgeon will then dilate the cervix and gently insert a suction device to remove the foetal matter.

What are the risks?

It is important to know that any surgical procedure involving the womb does carry a small risk of complications, such as infection, perforation or damage to the cervix, although it is rare for a previous termination of pregnancy to affect future fertility.

Research involving over 9,000 women has found no difference in fertility rates between those who had previously had a termination, compared with those who had not. Very rarely, heavy bleeding may occur which cannot be stopped. The surgeon may then be forced to carry out a hysterectomy to stop a life-threatening haemorrhage.

Antibiotics are usually given to cover the termination and reduce the chance of infection. If your blood group is Rhesus negative you will be given an injection of anti-D at the time of your operation. This will help to prevent you making anti-Rhesus antibodies (if the foetus is Rhesus positive), which might affect a future pregnancy.

Afterwards

After a termination you may feel some discomfort similar to bad period pains, which usually settles after a couple of days. There will usually be some mild bleeding, which often comes and goes before settling down into a brownish discharge, which may in turn last up to three weeks. Use sanitary pads, not tampons, during this time. Seek medical advice if the pain or bleeding does not settle or if you develop an offensive discharge or a fever.

Your first period will usually occur within four to six weeks. Most doctors advise you to refrain from sex for three weeks after a termination of pregnancy. It is a good idea to sort out a form of contraception as soon as possible, and before resuming your sex life.

Some women are so relieved at having had a termination that they do not have any adverse emotional problems afterwards. However, most women feel some sadness and some become very distressed and confused about what has happened. It is important to really think through all your options before going ahead with a termination to help avoid taking any actions that you might regret later. If you feel distressed after a termination, you can ask for counselling to help you through what is often a difficult time.

Resources

You can also contact the British Pregnancy Advisory Service who will offer practical advice on your options.

■ The above information is reprinted with kind permission from iVillage UK. Visit www.iVillage.co.uk for more information.

© iVillage

On what grounds are women having abortions?

Legal grounds for abortion	Number of abortions carried out on these grounds	Number of abortions carried out on these grounds as % of all abortions
A. The continuance of the pregnancy would involve risk to the life of the pregnant woman greater than if the pregnancy were terminated	137	0.08
B. The termination is necessary to prevent grave permanent injury to the physical or mental health of the pregnant woman	2,218	1.22
C. The continuance of the pregnancy would involve risk, greater than if the pregnancy were terminated, of injury to the physical or mental health of the pregnant woman	171,039	94.19
D. The continuance of the pregnancy would involve risk, greater than if the pregnancy were terminated, of injury to the physical or mental health of any existing child(ren) of the family of the pregnant woman	6,247	3.44
E. There is a substantial risk that if the child were born it would suffer from such physical or mental abnormalities as to be seriously handicapped	1,941	1.07
In an emergency, certified by one doctor as necessary: F. To save the life of the pregnant woman, or G. To prevent grave permanent injury to the physical or mental health of the pregnant woman	0	0

Source: Education For Choice (www.efc.org.uk). Data from the Department for Health for 2003. Crown copyright.

Abortion and depression

Abortion does not increase depression risk, study finds. By James Meikle

Aborting an unwanted foetus during a woman's first pregnancy does not increase her risk of depression and may actually make her less likely to suffer the blues, a report says today.

Researchers can find 'no credible evidence' to support the idea that termination poses a threat to a woman's mental health. Indeed, women who do not have an abortion are more likely to have had less education and income and come from larger families, all risk factors for depression.

'This suggests that if the goal is to reduce women's risk for depression, research should focus on how to prevent and ameliorate the effect of unwanted childbearing, particularly for younger women,' the researchers say in the online version of the *British Medical Journal*.

About two-thirds of the 185,000 abortions performed in England and Wales last year are thought to have involved women who were pregnant for the first time. BPAS, Britain's largest provider of abortion services, backed the conclusions by Nancy Russo of Arizona State University, and Sarah Schmiege of the University of Colorado. A spokeswoman said: 'We agree that abortion does not make you depressed. We offer free post-abortion counselling, and very few women take it up.'

The authors studied the history of more than 1,000 women, aged between 14 and 24 in 1979, who either aborted the foetus during their first pregnancy or chose to have the baby between 1970 and 1992.

The women were interviewed over several years to establish whether their decision was linked to later depression. The abortion group had a significantly higher education and income and lower total family size. The group with the highest risk of depression was that among women who went on to have their baby before 1980.

'Some women who undergo abortion will also experience clinical levels of depression. However, other research has found pre-existing mental health is the more important predictor of mental health after pregnancy, regardless of how the pregnancy is resolved.'

The anti-abortion group LIFE said it was concerned that the research suggested abortion carried no negative psychological consequences. Spokesman Matthew O'Gorman added: 'Such a study must be comprehensive and cover a much wider timeframe. We have women coming to see us who only started experiencing depression decades after the event.'
28 October 2005
© *Guardian Newspapers Limited 2006*

Dealing with an abortion

The decision to terminate a pregnancy is never easy, and can often give rise to mixed emotions. So how do you deal with it?

Coping with your emotions

While some women might feel relieved after terminating a pregnancy, it's also very common to feel sad, guilty, even confused, especially if you felt that at another time a baby would have been right for you. Depression and grief can also figure, and may be quite intense as your hormone levels drop back after the abortion. Try not to punish yourself, or worry that you have to go through any of this alone. Remember that they are your emotions and whatever you are feeling is fine.

Before the termination happened, you will have talked to two doctors about what to do for the best. You may have also discussed it with the father of the baby, members of your family, or a family planning counsellor. All this talking would have helped you come to the decision that an abortion was in your best interest, but no matter how often – or how hard – you thought about the situation, no one can predict how you'll feel afterwards.

Keep communicating

For many women who have been through the experience, the key is to keep on talking to all those people who've helped you this far. Don't be embarrassed that you're turning to them again, or worry they'll think you've made the wrong decision because you feel this way. They'll want to help. However, you may feel happier talking to someone outside the situation. If you want to talk in confidence to a post-abortion counsellor, call Brook Advisory Centres on 0800 0185023. They can be of help at any stage, no matter how long ago you had the abortion.

Take time

Some women take longer than others to get over terminating a pregnancy, whether it's two months, two years or longer. Everyone copes with their emotions in different ways. Some talk, others work it through on their own, but no matter how you feel, you have to face up to it, make sense of it, and deal it with it in a way that feels right to you.

Unplanned pregnancy is something nobody chooses to happen, so it's always wise to avoid risks and take precautions.

■   The above information is reprinted with kind permission from TheSite. org. Visit www.thesite.org for more information.

© *TheSite.org*

Abortion

Are you pregnant but not sure that you want to have a baby? Do you need more information about abortion?

This article will give you information about getting an abortion and what's involved. It's not an article about pregnancy choices. If you are undecided about whether to continue with the pregnancy, there are people you can talk to, to help you make a choice, but ultimately the decision is yours.

The majority of abortions (about 90%) are carried out before 13 weeks, and almost all (98%) before 20 weeks

---

Unplanned pregnancy is very common. About one in three pregnancies is unplanned and in one in five pregnancies the woman chooses to have an abortion. It can be a difficult choice to make and it can be a very emotional time. Talking to people you trust and making sure you have accurate information can help.

Is abortion legal?

Abortion, sometimes called termination of pregnancy (TOP), is legal in Britain under the Abortion Act 1967, as amended by the Human Fertilisation and Embryology Act 1990.

The Act says that two doctors must agree that an abortion would cause less damage to a woman's physical or mental health than continuing with the pregnancy. Most doctors feel that the distress of having to continue with an unwanted pregnancy is likely to be harmful to a woman's health. They will refer you for an abortion if you've decided you don't want a baby.

Abortion is legal in Northern Ireland in exceptional circumstances, but current guidance is unclear and many women in Northern Ireland find it difficult to get an abortion unless they travel to England. Women in Northern Ireland can contact fpa in Northern Ireland for confidential counselling, information and support on all the options available.

What is the legal time limit for abortion?

Abortion is legally available up to 24 weeks of pregnancy. It is safer when it is carried out in early pregnancy. Also, it can be difficult to get an abortion after 12 weeks of pregnancy so it's important to seek advice quickly, even if you're not sure you want an abortion.

The majority of abortions (about 90%) are carried out before 13 weeks, and almost all (98%) before 20 weeks.

The law says that abortion is legal after 24 weeks:

- if it is necessary to save the woman's life; or
- 'to prevent grave permanent injury to the physical or mental health of the pregnant woman', or
- if 'there is substantial risk that if the child were born it would suffer from such physical or mental abnormalities as to be seriously handicapped'.

Abortion after 24 weeks is extremely rare.

Weeks of pregnancy are usually worked out from the first day of your last normal menstrual period. When the stage of pregnancy is not clear, it can be checked using an ultrasound scan.

How do I go about getting an abortion?

Abortion care is available free through the NHS, or through private clinics and hospitals for a fee.

- NHS: you should see your GP or go to your local family planning or sexual health clinic. If the doctor you see does not refer women for abortion, they must refer you to another doctor. Most abortions are funded through the NHS but availability of NHS-funded abortions varies from area to area. The doctor or clinic will be able to advise you about local policy and services.
- Privately-run clinics: you can contact specialist abortion providers such as BPAS and Marie Stopes. You don't have to be referred by a doctor. These are non-profit-making charities that provide confidential abortion services. Current costs start from around £400 but vary, depending on the stage of pregnancy and the method of abortion. You may wish to contact them if you do not want to use the NHS or if you find that you are unable to obtain an NHS abortion. Many areas pay these charities to provide free NHS abortion services for their patients.

There are no private clinics in Scotland, only private hospitals, and the fee is around £1,500. You can contact fpa in Scotland for details.

What if I am uncertain about having an abortion?

The decision about whether to have an abortion or continue with a pregnancy is not an easy one to make.

Talking to friends and family can help or you might find it easier to talk to someone who is not so close to you. Your doctor may be able to refer you to a counsellor or you could contact one of the organisations listed on

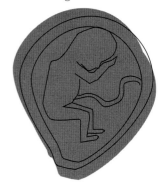

the fpa website. There are some other organisations that offer pregnancy testing and counselling but believe that abortion is morally wrong. They will not provide balanced information and will counsel you against it.

Will anyone else be told about my abortion?

Any woman who has an abortion, whatever age she is, has a right for that information to remain confidential.

Your partner, or the father of the child, has no legal rights

---

If you have any worries about confidentiality, discuss this with the doctor or nurse you speak to about your abortion. There is no legal requirement for your GP to know about your abortion. Many abortion services send a letter to your GP out of courtesy, to provide information in case you have any health problems after the abortion and to allow your medical records to be updated. Ask the hospital or clinic what they usually do and tell them if you do not want them to inform your GP.

If I am under 16, do I have to tell my parents?

No, you can have an abortion without telling your parents. The doctors will encourage you to involve your parents or another supportive adult, but if you choose not to, you can still have an abortion if both doctors believe that you fully understand what is involved and it is in your best interests.

This is called giving consent.

All information, advice and services are confidential, but health professionals are obliged, with your knowledge, to involve social services if they suspect you, or another young person, are at significant risk of harm (for example, sexual, emotional or physical abuse). This applies until you are 18 years old.

Do I need the agreement of my partner?

No. Your partner, or the father of the child, has no legal rights.

Many women do want to discuss the pregnancy with their partners and come to a joint decision, but you can go ahead with an abortion without your partner's knowledge or agreement. Where partners have tried to prevent an abortion by legal action, they have failed.

What can I do if my doctor won't refer me for an abortion?

If your doctor does not believe in abortion, they can refuse to help you but should always refer you to another doctor who will.

The General Medical Council's 'Duties of a Doctor' says that doctors must make sure that their personal beliefs do not affect patient care. If your doctor is not being helpful you could try and see another doctor at your general practice or visit a family planning clinic.

How long will I have to wait?

Waiting times vary according to where you live.

Ideally, once you have seen your GP or NHS clinic, or you have contacted a private clinic directly:

- You should be offered a first appointment at the hospital or clinic where your abortion will take place within five days, and never longer than 14 days. This is to confirm your pregnancy, your eligibility for abortion and the procedures.
- The abortion should be within one week of this first visit and you should never wait for more than two weeks.
- As a minimum standard, you should not have to wait more than three weeks from your first

contact with your GP or clinic to the time of your abortion.

Women who have other medical problems may have to wait longer as they may need more specialist advice.

Where will my abortion take place?

Abortions are carried out in either NHS hospitals or specialist clinics that are licensed and approved. For most women an abortion is a day-care procedure that does not involve an overnight stay.

What should happen before the abortion?

During your first appointment you should be given:

- an opportunity to talk things through, if you want to;
- information about the different methods of abortion, which is suitable for your stage of pregnancy, and where they are carried out;
- information on any possible risks or complications relating to the abortion;
- a blood test to check your blood group and for anaemia;
- a consent form to sign.

You should also be offered tests to detect chlamydia or other sexually-transmitted infections, or be given antibiotics. This is to prevent infection after the abortion.

The doctor or nurse will also ask you questions about your medical history to ensure that you are offered a suitable abortion method.

You may:

- need to have an ultrasound scan, but this is not always necessary. If it is, it should not normally be carried out where you will meet women who intend to continue with their pregnancies;
- have a vaginal examination;
- be offered a cervical smear test if appropriate;
- Be offered a chance to discuss which contraception you may wish to use after the abortion.

What happens during the abortion?

There are different abortion procedures and the method used depends on how long you have been pregnant.

An abortion service should ideally be able to offer a choice of abortion methods, if appropriate.

Early medical abortion (up to nine weeks of pregnancy)

This type of abortion is like an early natural miscarriage. After your first assessment visit, you will need two appointments on two separate days. You should be able to carry out your usual activities between appointments. On the first visit, you will be given a tablet(s) called mifepristone to block the pregnancy hormone that is necessary for the pregnancy to continue.

On the second visit (usually two days later), prostaglandin tablets are taken by mouth or put into your vagina. This causes the womb to expel the pregnancy, which usually happens during the next four to six hours. This method of abortion is becoming more widely available in clinics and hospitals.

Vacuum aspiration or suction termination (usually from seven to 15 weeks of pregnancy)

Some services may offer suction termination up to 15 weeks, while others use this method up to about 12 weeks. Sometimes this method can be used before seven weeks but this is not common. The procedure takes five to 10 minutes and can be carried out under a local anaesthetic (given around the area of the entrance to the womb), or a general anaesthetic, or under conscious sedation. Conscious sedation is when you are given drugs that make you sleepy. This means that you won't remember everything that happens during the abortion but you will stay conscious during the procedure.

The passage through the cervix (entrance to the womb) is dilated – gently stretched and opened – until it is wide enough to allow the contents of the womb to be removed with a small suction tube. To make this safer the cervix may be softened, with a tablet placed in the vagina, a few hours before the abortion. You will usually go home on the same day.

Medical abortion (after nine weeks of pregnancy)

The drugs used for early medical abortion are also used for abortion later in pregnancy. The difference is that later in pregnancy the abortion takes longer and you may need to have more than one dose of the prostaglandin drug. The abortion is like having a late natural miscarriage. The abortion process is usually quick enough for you to return home the same day but sometimes it is necessary to stay at the clinic or hospital overnight, particularly for abortions performed later in pregnancy.

Surgical dilation and evacuation (D&E) (from about 15 weeks of pregnancy)

The cervix is gently stretched and dilated and the pregnancy is removed in fragments using forceps and a suction tube. This takes 10 to 20 minutes and usually needs a general anaesthetic. You may be able to return home the same day if you are healthy and there are no complications.

Abortion after 21 weeks

Abortion at this stage is not common. It involves either the surgical dilation and evacuation method, or the medical abortion method described above. Whichever method is used a doctor will ensure the heart of the foetus is stopped so it is not born alive. You will normally need to spend one night in the clinic or hospital.

Is abortion painful?

Whatever method of abortion is chosen, you will have some period-type pain or discomfort.

You should be offered and advised about appropriate painkillers for this.

Is abortion safe?

For most women an abortion is safer than having a baby. Abortion is not entirely risk-free, but problems are less likely to occur when abortion is performed early in pregnancy, when local anaesthetic is used and steps are taken to reduce the risk of infection. You should be advised of any possible complications relating to the type of abortion you will have and the stage of pregnancy you have reached.

Are there risks at the time of the abortion?

Problems at the time of the abortion are not very common but are more likely to occur the later in the pregnancy you have an abortion.

- Excessive bleeding (haemorrhage) happens in around one in every 1,000 abortions.
- Damage to the cervix happens in no more than 10 in every 1,000 abortions.
- Damage to the womb at the time of surgical abortion happens in up to four in every 1,000 abortions.
- Damage to the womb happens in fewer than one in every 1,000 medical abortions done between 12 and 24 weeks (a time known as mid-trimester).

Are there risks after the abortion?

Infection is the most common problem after abortion. Usually this is caused by a pre-existing infection. You are most likely to get an infection in the two weeks after the abortion. Taking antibiotics at the time of the abortion helps to reduce this risk.

Most infections are easy to treat. If not treated, you could get a more severe infection of the reproductive organs (pelvic inflammatory disease or PID) which could lead to infertility in the future and ectopic pregnancy (a dangerous pregnancy outside the womb, usually in the fallopian tube).

In some cases the abortion may fail to remove the pregnancy. This isn't harmful, as long as it is recognised at the time, it just means that you will need further treatment. This is more common with medical abortion or very early surgical abortion (less than seven weeks).

The doctor or nurse will tell you what symptoms to look out for after the abortion. You should see your doctor or nurse as soon as possible if you have any of the following as they may be symptoms of an infection or suggest that the abortion has failed:

- pain in your lower abdomen;
- vaginal discharge, particularly if it is abnormal or smells;
- persistent bleeding;
- feeling unwell;
- a temperature or fever.

- Information is taken from the fpa factsheet 'Abortion' and is reprinted with permission. Visit www.fpa.org.uk for more information.

© fpa

For men

Information from Education For Choice

Introduction

Because pregnancy, childbirth and parenting have such an enormous impact on a woman's life, men often feel that they do not have a role to play in the decisions that need to be made about pregnancy. However, many men want to express their feelings, to offer their support and to be involved in the decisions about their partner's pregnancy.

Whilst professionals must ensure that women are supported to make the decision that's right for them, there is increasing recognition that men can and should be involved as much as is possible in the choices and decisions that pregnancy entails.

Men's rights and pregnancy

Men have the right to avoid conceiving unplanned pregnancies either by choosing not to have sex or to use condoms: currently condoms are the only form of contraception over which a man can take full responsibility.

Beyond this, men have few rights in a decision about their partner's pregnancy because the law makes no other provision.

- If a woman chooses to continue with a pregnancy he may be held financially responsible for

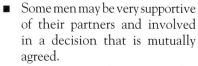

the upbringing of the child, regardless of their relationship or his part in the child's life.
- If she chooses to have an abortion she may do so without his agreement.

Men's rights and abortion

Her partner may be the first person a woman turns to when she discovers she is pregnant and so his views may very well influence her decision. However, under UK law he has no legal right to make her have an abortion or to prevent her from having one. Instead, any decision to have an abortion must be approved by two doctors who agree with the woman that it is in her best interests to have one.

Involving men in pregnancy decision-making

Men's experiences of involvement in decisions about pregnancy vary widely.

- Some men may be very supportive of their partners and involved in a decision that is mutually agreed.
- Some men may have no involvement because she may choose not to inform him that she is pregnant or to include him in any decisions regarding it.
- Some men, sometimes through coercion or abuse, may become the sole decision-makers.

Reasons why some men are consulted and involved

Couples in a happy, committed relationship may feel more able to talk to each other about their feelings, opinions and anxieties.

Most men accept that the final decision about pregnancy should rest with the woman, but need an opportunity to express their feelings about the pregnancy

---

They may have talked about their current circumstances and how children could impact on their lives.

They may have discussed their hopes for the future and talked about how and when children fit this picture.

A woman may feel more confident in involving her partner if they both understand that when faced with unplanned pregnancy, and an unsure outcome, that it is not possible to compromise – so someone must make that final decision.

Most people accept that because the woman will be more directly affected by the pregnancy, she is the best person to make the final decision, having listened to her partner's thoughts and feelings.

... WE NEED TO TALK ABOUT THE TWO—

—OR THE THREE OF US...

Reasons why some men are not involved

Some women are anxious to conceal pregnancy if they feel they will be blamed or punished by their partner for failing to use contraception effectively.

Women who become pregnant as a result of casual sex might choose not to tell the man she has become pregnant at all.

Women who are pregnant as a result of rape may not want to, or be able to, communicate with the man responsible.

A woman who is undecided about her pregnancy might feel that she is very vulnerable to pressure from other people

---

Some women do not believe that the man has any right to participate in the decision about pregnancy as it is her body that is affected by the pregnancy.

Some women are discouraged from involving their partners by family or friends, if for example they disapprove of him.

Reasons why some men are the sole decision-makers

Sometimes a man who is having an abusive or incestuous sexual relationship with a woman might use the threat of violence to make her choose an abortion or to prevent her from having one.

Sometimes family members may prevent a woman from having an abortion or try to force her into one because of their ideas about pregnancy, sex outside of marriage or abortion.

Fear of intimidation or violence within a relationship can make it increasingly difficult for a woman to act on her right to make a decision about either sex or pregnancy, leading the man to become the sole decision-maker. Recent evidence suggests that the incidence and severity of domestic violence often increases when a woman becomes pregnant.

Why a woman might be anxious about involving her partner

A woman who is undecided about her pregnancy might feel that she is very vulnerable to pressure from other people and might want to talk to a professional to clarify her own thoughts and feelings before she talks to her partner or family.

She might think she already knows what her partner will think and say about the pregnancy.

She might think he will not be supportive of her decision.

Why men want to be involved in making the decision

Most men accept that the final decision about pregnancy should rest with the woman, but need an opportunity to express their feelings about the pregnancy. If a man has a chance to say how he feels he might feel satisfied that his partner understands and has heard his feelings and can take them into account as she makes her decision.

It might be that both partners feel the same way about the pregnancy, in which case the woman will find her partner a good source of support.

Even when they are not agreed about whether or not to proceed with a pregnancy it can be helpful to hear each others' opinions. Hearing a woman's reasons for continuing with her pregnancy or ending it can help her partner to sympathise with her situation and dilemma and give him a better insight into her thoughts and feelings. This may enable him to support her in her decision, even if it isn't what he would have wanted her to do.

How can men support their partners?

- Listen to your partner. Almost everyone will have an opinion about her pregnancy. Make sure she's had a chance to express her thoughts.
- Help her to think through the pros and cons of the pregnancy.
- Let her know what you think and feel.
- Make sure she goes to an appropriate agency that will help her to make up her own mind about the pregnancy, free of pressure.
- Accompany her to speak to her GP or family planning clinic so that she can talk to a professional. Remember that most professionals will want to spend some time talking to her on her own.
- Help her break the news of her pregnancy to other family members if she is worried about their response.
- Encourage her to make the decision that is right for her.
- Find out relevant information about her options.
- Be realistic about what support you are able to give her.

- The above information is reprinted with kind permission from Education For Choice. For more information, visit www.efc.org.uk.
© *Education For Choice*

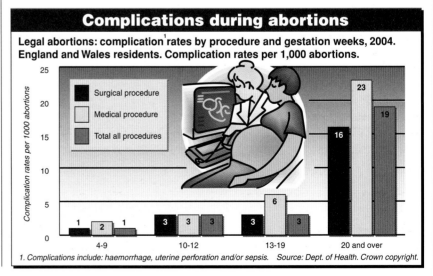

Complications during abortions

Legal abortions: complication[1] rates by procedure and gestation weeks, 2004. England and Wales residents. Complication rates per 1,000 abortions.

(Bar chart: Complication rates per 1000 abortions)

Legend:
- Surgical procedure
- Medical procedure
- Total all procedures

Values by gestation weeks:
- 4-9: 1, 2, 1
- 10-12: 3, 3, 3
- 13-19: 3, 6, 3
- 20 and over: 16, 23, 19

1. Complications include: haemorrhage, uterine perforation and/or sepsis.   Source: Dept. of Health. Crown copyright.

Real life: abortion

Information from RUThinking?

Nicky's story

I was 18 and had been seeing James for four months. We went away to a weekend party and I forgot to take my contraceptive pills with me. I missed two in a row. The night of the party we had sex. I knew we should use protection but I just hoped it would be alright instead.

I should have taken emergency contraception the next day, but I just kept my fingers crossed and took the rest of the pills in the packet. I didn't really think about it again until I was a week late for my period, but I put it down to exam stress.

I wasn't ready for a baby. My ambitions and social life would have to go on hold. My friends would be out having fun while I sat at home with a baby

After another week I got freaked. My breasts were tender and my tummy was bloated. I decided to take a pregnancy test. The home testing kit was positive, but to double check I went to my local Brook for a free test. James came with me and helped me keep it together.

The doctor confirmed I was six to eight weeks pregnant and asked what I wanted to do. I wasn't ready for a baby. My ambitions and social life would have to go on hold. My friends would be out having fun while I sat at home with a baby.

I asked the doctor if I could terminate the pregnancy and she agreed to refer me to the local hospital.

James looked pretty shocked. I wasn't sure how I felt; it was a mixture of panic, nerves and anticipation. Later we talked and decided we were doing the right thing.

I had to wait a couple of weeks for the appointment at the hospital clinic. I took a friend for moral support.

The doctor asked me why I wanted an abortion, so I explained my reasons and he seemed to agree with me. I didn't realise that a doctor can refuse an abortion, though I think that's pretty rare.

I had an internal examination, which was pretty embarrassing, but painless.

A nurse talked to me about the procedure and what contraception I should use in the future. I was offered counselling too.

I had the abortion a couple of weeks later. James stayed with me until I was taken to the ward and after the anaesthetic I don't remember a thing.

Afterwards, I wasn't in too much pain – it just felt like bad period cramps.

At 2pm the doctor came to check my sanitary pad which was gross. After that I was allowed to leave.

I felt tired for a couple of days and was bleeding, but not very heavily.

I had to visit my GP a few weeks later for a check up, but everything was fine.

I felt quite emotional. I didn't regret the decision, but the changes in my hormones now I'd stopped being pregnant were making me moody, a bit like before my period.

The doctor asked me why I wanted an abortion, so I explained my reasons and he seemed to agree with me. I didn't realise that a doctor can refuse an abortion

Overall I felt a huge sense of relief and really sure I had made the right decision.

I'm 23 now and James and I are living together. I got my degree and have a great new job.

If I got pregnant now I could cope with the responsibility, but I will never regret the choice I made.

James's story

I didn't know much about contraception when I first started having sex. I was just interested in having a good time.

At 18 I was having fun and seeing the girl of my dreams. Nicky was brilliant.

When we started having sex we decided it would just be easier if Nicky went on the pill. Easier for me anyway.

When she told me she was pregnant I was stunned and confused. My feelings ranged from totally freaked to kind of excited. I loved Nicola, but I wasn't ready to be a dad

---

One weekend we went away and Nicola forgot to take her pills. We didn't really worry too much as it was only two days of her missing the pill.

When she told me she was pregnant I was stunned and confused. My feelings ranged from totally freaked to kind of excited. I loved Nicola, but I wasn't ready to be a dad. We were both doing well at college and knew that a baby would change things completely. Still, I promised I would stick by her whatever she decided.

I went with Nicky to get the pregnancy confirmed at a clinic. I wasn't allowed to go in and see the nurse with her, which was weird as they were talking about stuff that could change my life forever.

After Nicky had the pregnancy confirmed at the clinic we talked it through, but she had decided that she wanted an abortion.

The abortion happened about two weeks later. I took Nicky to hospital and when we got to the ward I had to leave. It was really hard to walk away.

A few hours later I went back to the hospital with a big bunch of flowers. Nicky was waiting for me looking really tired and pale.

For the next couple of days I stayed at her place and looked after her. She had told her parents about the abortion and they were really supportive. I didn't want to tell mine and still haven't. Maybe I will one day.

I'm 23 now and I've got a degree. Nicky and I are saving to go travelling in the next couple of years. Money's still a bit tight but its nothing compared to if we'd had a kid!

We will never forget the abortion, but we both know we made the best decision we could. We'll make great parents one day, but for now we keep using those condoms!

For more information and resources about abortion, visit the Education For Choice website which is dedicated to enabling young people to make informed choices about pregnancy and abortion.

■ The above information is reprinted with kind permission from RUThinking? Visit www.ruthinking.co.uk for more information.

© *RUThinking?*

Abortion statistics

Information from Brook

In 2005, the latest full year for which statistics are available, 186,400 abortions took place in England and Wales. That's a rate of 17.8 per thousand women aged 15 to 44.

In Scotland, during the same period, there were 12,600 abortions resulting in an abortion rate of 11.9 per thousand women aged 15 to 44.

The majority of abortions are performed under 13 weeks of pregnancy. In England and Wales in 2005 67% were carried out under 10 weeks of pregnancy and 23% were carried out between 10 and 12 weeks. During the same period 1% of terminations occurred at 20 weeks or later.

In Scotland 67% were carried out under 10 weeks of pregnancy and 26% were carried out between 10 and 13 weeks. Less than 1% were carried out at 20 weeks or more.

Abortion rates are highest amongst women aged under 24. In 2005 the rate of abortions per thousand 15 to 19-year-olds in England and Wales was 23 and in 20 to 24-year-olds it was also 32. In Scotland the abortion rate per thousand 16 to 19-year-olds was 23, and in 20 to 24-year-olds it was 22.

There are wide variations in access to abortion services. A survey by Voice for Choice found that the percentage of abortions performed or funded by the NHS in England in 2002 varied between primary care trusts from 46% to 96%.

There are also wide variations in the waiting times for abortion. In some parts of the country the same survey found women waiting up to five weeks or more to get an appointment.

■ The above information is reprinted with kind permission from Brook. Brook provides free and confidential sexual health advice and services specifically for young people under 25. For further information, visit www.brook.org.uk or contact the Young People's Information Service by calling 0800 0185 023 or texting BROOK HELP to 81222.

© *Brook Advisory Centres*

Global Gag Rule

Information from the International Planned Parenthood Federation

First introduced in 1984 and reintroduced by President George W. Bush in 2001, the Global Gag Rule (also known as the Mexico City Policy) puts non-governmental organisations from outside the United States in an untenable position, forcing them to choose between carrying out their work safeguarding the health and rights of women or losing their funding from the US.

In 2006 alone an estimated 19 million women will undergo an unsafe abortion; nearly 70,000 of them will pay for it with their lives

The Gag Rule prohibits organisations in receipt of US funds from using their own money to provide abortion information, services and care, or even discussing abortion or criticising unsafe abortion.

It even prevents organisations from working on these issues at the request of their own governments.

The Gag Rule severely restricts freedom of speech; it interferes with the doctor-client relationship; and hinders balanced consideration of liberalising abortion laws based on public health concerns and human rights.

Around the world this has had a dramatic impact on the ability of our member associations, and many other organisations, which have rejected the Gag Rule, and consequently lost much of their funding, to provide full sexual and reproductive health services.

The policy has restricted the freedom of speech and association of those organisations who are bound by its regulations. However, anti-abortion advocacy is allowed, underscoring the ideological nature of the Gag Rule.

The Gag Rule fails in its stated intent to reduce the global incidence of abortion. Rather, by dramatically impairing the delivery of sexual and reproductive health services, its actual impact has been to increase the number of unintended pregnancies and the abortions that inevitably follow.

Our member associations, working around the world, must deal with the consequences of unsafe abortion every day. In 2006 alone an estimated 19 million women will undergo an unsafe abortion; nearly 70,000 of them will pay for it with their lives. Millions more will suffer injuries,

Kenya and the Global Gag Rule

IPPF's member association in Kenya, Family Health Options Kenya (FHOK), provides a significant share of the country's contraceptive and reproductive health services.

Faced with a choice between losing all its funding and technical aid from the US Agency for International Development and stopping all its work on safe abortion, FHOK chose to forfeit the aid to be free to advocate for the health and well-being of Kenyan women.

The resulting loss of funding saw the closure of three FHOK clinics, the scaling back of services in its remaining clinics and the slashing of funding to outreach programmes. This has made it much harder for poor Kenyans to access family planning services and information, and must inevitably lead to more unwanted pregnancies and unsafe abortions.

illness or disability resulting from unsafe abortion.

The public health and human rights impact of unsafe abortion have been ignored by the international community for too long. The Millennium Development Goals have renewed the focus on global development issues. Our abortion report: *Death and Denial* seeks to move that focus onto the lives of the millions of women who are forced to put their lives at risk from unsafe abortion every year.

■ The above information is reprinted with kind permission from the International Planned Parenthood Federation. Visit www.ippf.org for more information.

© *IPPF*

Statistics from the International Planned Parenthood Federation report *Death and Denial: Unsafe Abortion and Poverty*, January 2006.

Abortion-related hospitalisations

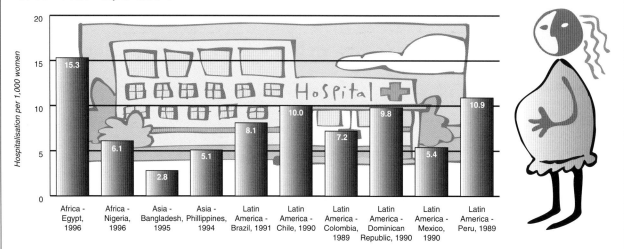

Source: Alan Guttmacher Institute, Sharing Responsibility; Women, Society and Abortion Worldwide

All abortions by global region

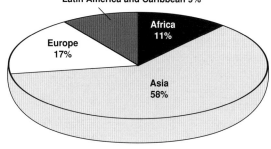

Latin America and Caribbean 9%
Africa 11%
Europe 17%
Asia 58%

Unsafe abortion in developing countries

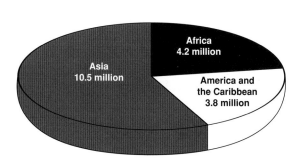

Africa 4.2 million
Asia 10.5 million
America and the Caribbean 3.8 million

Source: Alan Guttmacher Institute, Sharing Responsibility; Women, Society and Abortion Worldwide

Grounds on which abortion is permitted around the world

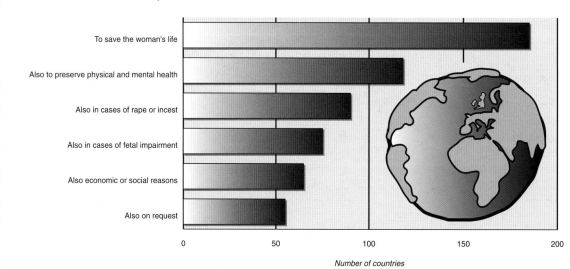

- To save the woman's life
- Also to preserve physical and mental health
- Also in cases of rape or incest
- Also in cases of fetal impairment
- Also economic or social reasons
- Also on request

Number of countries

Source: World Health Report 2005, World Health Organization.

Ethical consideration

From the British Medical Association briefing paper 'The law and ethics of abortion'

Moral arguments

People generally take one of three main stances on abortion: pro-abortion, anti-abortion and the middle ground that abortion is acceptable in some circumstances. The main arguments for each of these positions is set out below.

Arguments used in support of abortion

Those who support the wide availability of abortion consider that abortion is not wrong in itself and need not involve undesirable consequences. These arguments tend not to recognise foetal rights or to acknowledge the foetus to be a person. According to some, abortion is a matter of a woman's right to exercise control over her own body. Moralists who judge actions by their consequences alone could argue that abortion is equivalent to a deliberate failure to conceive a child and since contraception is widely available, abortion should be too. Some think that even if the foetus is a person, its rights are very limited and do

not weigh significantly against the interests of people who have already been born, such as parents or existing children of the family. The interests of society at large might outweigh any right accorded to the foetus in some circumstances, such as if, for example, overpopulation or famine threatened that society. In such cases, abortion might be seen by some people as moving from a neutral act to one which should be encouraged. Similarly, utilitarians who see a duty to promote the greatest happiness and maximise the number of worthwhile lives, could argue that there should be as few as possible unwanted children in the world.

Most people who support this position do so on the basis that the

overriding principle is the woman's right to choose what happens to her body. This use of the language of 'choice' conveys approval regardless of the type of pressures the individual faces and any constraints on her freedom to make a genuine choice.

Those who consider that an embryo, from the moment of conception, is a human being with full moral status, see abortion as killing in the same sense as the murder of any other person

---

Arguments used against abortion

Some people consider that abortion is wrong in any circumstances because it fails to recognise the rights of the foetus or because it challenges the notion of the sanctity of all human life. Some argue that permitting abortion diminishes the respect society feels for other vulnerable humans, possibly leading to their involuntary euthanasia. Those who consider that an embryo, from the moment of conception, is a human being with full moral status, see abortion as killing in the same sense as the murder of any other person. Those who take this view cannot accept that women should be allowed to obtain abortion without legal repercussions, however difficult the lives of those women or their existing families are made as a result.

Such views may be based on religious or moral convictions that each human life has unassailable intrinsic value, which is not dim-

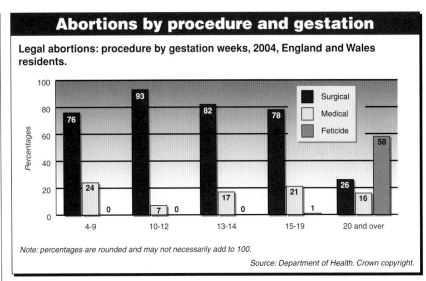

Abortions by procedure and gestation

Legal abortions: procedure by gestation weeks, 2004, England and Wales residents.

Legend: Surgical, Medical, Feticide

Note: percentages are rounded and may not necessarily add to 100.

Source: Department of Health. Crown copyright.

inished by any impairment or suffering that may be involved for the individual living that life. It is also argued that abortion treats humans merely as a means to an end in that abortion can be seen as a discarding of a foetus in which the pregnant woman no longer has any interest. Many worry that the availability of abortion on grounds of foetal abnormality encourages prejudice towards any person with a handicap and insidiously creates the impression that the only valuable people are those who conform to some ill-defined stereotype of 'normality'.

Some people who oppose abortion in general, concede that it may be justifiable in very exceptional cases such as where it is the result of rape or the consequence of exploitation of a young girl or a mentally incompetent woman. Risk to the mother's life may be another justifiable exception but only where abortion is the only option. It would thus not be seen as justifiable to abort a foetus if the life of both foetus and mother could be saved by any other solution.

Arguments used to support abortion in some circumstances

Many people argue that abortion may be justified in a greater number of circumstances than those conceded by anti-abortionists but that it would be undesirable to allow abortion on demand. To do so might incur undesirable effects, such as encouraging irresponsible attitudes to contraception. It could also lead to a devaluation of the lives of viable foetuses and trivialise the potential psychological effects of abortion on women and on health professionals.

These types of argument are based on the premise that the embryo starts off without rights, although having a special status from conception in view of its potential for development, and that it acquires rights and status throughout its development. The notion of developing foetal rights and practical factors, such as the possible distress to the pregnant woman, nurses, doctors or other children in the family, gives rise to the view that early abortion is more acceptable than late abortion.

According to some, abortion is a matter of a woman's right to exercise control over her own body

---

Some people support this position on pragmatic grounds, believing that abortions will always be sought by women who are desperate and that it is better for society to provide abortion services which are safe and which can be monitored and regulated, rather than to allow 'back-street' practices.

The BMA's view on abortion

In the 1970s and 1980s the BMA approved policy statements supporting the 1967 Abortion Act as 'a practical and humane piece of legislation' and calling for its expansion to Northern Ireland. The BMA does not consider that abortion is unethical, but as with any act having profound moral implications, the justifications must be commensurate with the consequences. The BMA's advice to its members is to act within the boundaries of the law and of their own conscience. Patients are, however, entitled to receive objective medical advice regardless of their doctor's personal views for or against abortion. Furthermore, a doctor could be sued for damages if, because of a failure to refer, a delay is caused which results in the woman being unable to obtain a termination.

Foetal pain

Whether, and at what stage, a foetus feels pain has been a matter of much recent debate and past practice has been partly influenced by Department of Health advice. Interpretation of the evidence on foetal pain is conflicting, with some arguing that the foetus has the potential to feel pain at 10 weeks' gestation, others arguing that it is unlikely to feel pain before 26 weeks' gestation and still others arguing for some unspecified gestational period inbetween.

There is clearly a need for further research to provide more conclusive evidence about the experiences and sensations of the foetus *in utero*. In the meantime the BMA recommends that, when carrying out any surgical procedures (whether an abortion or a therapeutic intervention) on the foetus *in utero*, due consideration must be given to appropriate measures for minimising the risk of pain. This should include an assessment of the most recent evidence available. Even if there is no incontrovertible evidence that foetuses feel pain the use of pain relief, when carrying out invasive procedures, may help to relieve the anxiety of the parents and of health professionals.

■ The above information is reprinted with kind permission from the British Medical Association. Visit www.bma.org.uk for more information.

© *British Medical Association 2006*

Abortion: the answer to unplanned pregnancy?

Almost half of all pregnancies are unplanned and during their lifetime one in three British women will have an abortion, as reported in Channel 4's programme *My Foetus*

By Jo Carlowe

In 2002 184,993 women had abortions in Britain. The figures are astounding, especially given the existence of 14 different methods of contraception and the publication of the National Strategy of Sexual Health in 2001, in which the government promised to tackle the problem.

So what is going wrong? Is the message about contraception not getting through or are the available methods unreliable? And what happens when a woman is faced with an unplanned pregnancy – is impartial advice, accessible services and adequate support available or can she anticipate harsh judgements, patchy services and limited choice?

Sexual health experts say the answers are complex. When looking at the high abortion rate, Tony Kerridge, spokesperson for Marie Stopes International (MSI), says economic factors play a part – fewer people can afford to keep a child conceived by accident.

'The cost of childcare has risen dramatically. Combined with the rising costs of mortgages, which often dictate that both partners need to be in full-time employment, such factors may play a decisive part in decisions about when, or even if, to start a family.'

> **'The prudish British attitude makes it difficult for people to seek advice. Sex needs to be less stigmatised'**

The fpa (formerly the Family Planning Association) says the problem is also cultural – we British aren't terribly good at talking about sex. There's a reticence right across the board from educators through to health professionals – as a result most people know a fraction of the available facts, and where information is available it is not always impartial.

'The prudish British attitude makes it difficult for people to seek advice. Sex needs to be less stigmatised,' says an fpa spokesperson. 'The need for information is constant – from school and throughout adult life.'

Young people agree – a recent survey showed that 62 per cent of 18 to 24-year-olds said they did not have enough information about the risks of unprotected sex.

MSI would like to see compulsory comprehensive sex and life skills education on the National Curriculum. In addition, the organisation wants family planning advice to be more accessible – preferably through specialist centres in schools and youth clubs. Currently 82 per cent of women get family planning information from their GP surgery.

'Young people have consistently said that they do not like seeking out family planning advice from their family GP,' says Kerridge.

Moreover, GP consultation times are limited and as a result many doctors only offer one or two favoured inexpensive methods of contraception.

'Newer, more effective methods such as contraceptive implants, patches and injections tend to be more expensive to prescribe for budget conscious practitioners,' says Kerridge.

And yet these methods could reduce the number of unplanned pregnancies. People want both information – the fpa receives 100,000 inquiries a year from callers seeking contraceptive advice – and to use contraception. In fact, only 3 per cent of women with unplanned pregnancies have used no contraception. One-fifth of unplanned pregnancies are due to condom failure and nearly two-

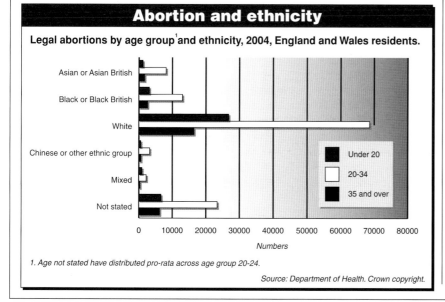

Abortion and ethnicity

Legal abortions by age group[1] and ethnicity, 2004, England and Wales residents.

Asian or Asian British
Black or Black British
White
Chinese or other ethnic group
Mixed
Not stated

Under 20
20-34
35 and over

0   10000   20000   30000   40000   50000   60000   70000   80000

Numbers

1. Age not stated have distributed pro-rata across age group 20-24.

Source: Department of Health. Crown copyright.

thirds because of problems with the pill. Around a quarter of women on the pill say they miss at least one a month – these women are not always told about alternative methods such as contraceptive patches.

There is also some ignorance about the methods of emergency contraception that are available. In 2002-2003 five per cent of women used the 'morning after pill' and only one per cent had an emergency IUD fitted (a contraceptive device fitted inside the uterus which can prevent pregnancy if inserted up to five days after having sex).

Even assuming a woman qualifies for an abortion, she then faces an 'NHS lottery'. In Kingston and Richmond in London, only half of all abortions are NHS-funded compared to 90 per cent in Coventry

---

The fpa wants emergency contraceptive pills to be made available in advance to women, a move termed 'access through the bathroom cabinet'. Some women already obtain these pills in advance by pretending that they have had unprotected sex and could be pregnant.

Deception in relation to sexual health is nothing new. For decades women have been forced to be surreptitious about their sexual practices. When in 1803 abortion was made a criminal offence – with a penalty of up to life imprisonment – women opted for backstreet abortions. By the time the Abortion Act 1967 legalised terminations, it is thought 120,000 women a year had resorted to this desperate measure.

Even today (unlike in other European countries) abortion is still not available on request. Instead two doctors must give their written consent before the abortion can proceed.

MSI calls this law 'archaic' and is lobbying for legislation to enable abortion on request in the first trimester (up to 14 weeks).

Even assuming a woman qualifies for an abortion, she then faces an 'NHS lottery'. In Kingston and Richmond in London, only half of all abortions are NHS-funded compared to 90 per cent in Coventry. In 2001, 79 per cent of women in north-east Lincolnshire obtained an abortion before 10 weeks compared to just 26 per cent in Great Yarmouth. The government's Sexual Health Strategy specifies that women shouldn't wait for more than three weeks from consultation to having an abortion but 27 per cent of primary care trusts have waiting times of 35 days or more. This can mean the difference between a simple procedure and a more complex invasive one. The fpa wants waiting times reduced to 72 hours from the first consultation.

MSI would like to see additional legislation permitting nurse practitioners (as opposed to doctors) to provide first trimester non-general anaesthetic abortion procedures to help reduce waiting times.

However, for some women abortion will always be taboo. If they can't keep the child then adoption is the only option. It is a choice that is not always presented and seldom taken. Experts estimate that as few as 100 unplanned pregnancies a year end in adoption.

Kerridge of MSI, says adoption is a difficult choice for women because of the 'overt visibility of a continued pregnancy when compared to the privacy of an abortion.'

The British Association for Adoption and Fostering (BAAF) would like to see information on adoption made available in antenatal clinics and GP surgeries.

Whatever decision is made, it is one that is rarely taken lightly. People faced with an unexpected pregnancy need better access to services and greater support. More crucially, the information gap needs to be tackled. A greater readiness to discuss rather than walk away from the topic of sexual health could arm people with the knowledge they need to avoid ever going through the emotional wringer of an unplanned pregnancy.
Last updated June 2005

■ The above information is reprinted with kind permission from channel4.com. Visit www.channel4.com for more information.
© channel4.com

The new pro-lifers

The rise in infertility has given a huge boost to the anti-abortion movement

By Cristina Odone

The stereotype of the anti-abortion activist was never particularly accurate. Victoria Gillick, fired by religious zeal and with a brood of children clinging to her apron strings, made for great copy and televisual images; but even back in the early 1980s pro-life campaigns drew young professionals as well as Catholic morality mums. The new pro-lifers are different. They aren't freaks or fanatics; they are probably your neighbours. They may not volunteer to stuff envelopes or hand out leaflets for traditional anti-abortion organisations such as LIFE and SPUC (the Society for the Protection of the Unborn Child). They don't evangelise and they certainly don't intimidate. They don't even regard abortion as a 'sin'. This new wave of pro-lifers hate abortion because they hate the waste of an egg. They are among Britain's growing number of infertile couples who, after years trying for a baby, and many cycles of IVF treatment, know just how precious that egg can be.

Pro-lifers in Britain were always different from their US counterparts. The murder of abortionists and fire-bombing of family-planning clinics were never adopted as tactics here. Intimidation via the Internet, whereby people are targeted with hate messages (and often find their address and phone number listed for all the stalkers to read), has recently been imported from America by outfits such as the UK Life League. But James Dowson, the tattooed Orangeman who heads the UK Life League, boasts only a handful of followers, and his influence on the pro-life movement is scarcely felt – LIFE, SPUC and CORE (Comment on Reproductive Ethics) reject outright the use of violence in their work.

Dowson, whose targets include a Catholic girls' school that offers sex education, made headlines this week. But he and his ilk will always be on the fringe of the anti-abortion movement. It is the new recruits who will bring the pro-life cause centre stage. Their presence may be difficult to quantify but, as Martin Foley of LIFE notes, 'the rise in infertility represents a very powerful factor in today's pro-life movement'.

> ### For the 45,000 British couples who seek fertility treatment annually, the 200,000 terminations that take place each year are a personal insult

Dowson's evangelical zeal to punish the sinners who murder an innocent life elicits little sympathy in a secular society. Far more powerful, to contemporary minds, is the appeal that the infertile pro-lifer projects: abortion as ingratitude. Infertility is now so much part of our culture that we are bound to know someone whose repeated tries for a baby have moved us to tears. Whatever our own convictions, it is hard not to share their revulsion for abortion as life snubbed. Who has not imagined, while stroking baby's head or watching their child play, what life would be like if they had not been possible?

For the 45,000 British couples who seek fertility treatment annually, the 200,000 terminations that take place each year are a personal insult: how dare anyone discard something that you yearn for so greatly? The woman who opts to abort has what you can't have – unless you spend a lot of money (£2,000 per cycle), risk potential health hazards and ride an emotional rollercoaster – is getting rid of the very object for which you are undergoing a series of painful injections and undignified examinations. She takes an hour or so to free herself of the foetus; you take months, years of successive cycles, to (maybe) create a new life. The envy that the barren feel for the fertile boils over into hatred when the proof of that fertility is cast off like a pair of dirty knickers.

For couples seeking assistance with conception, and for the 30,000 women who know they cannot have children naturally, the argument that legal abortion empowers the sisterhood holds little sway. Feminism, as has often been the case, becomes a casualty of fertility. It is horrible to think of the poor, ignorant or oppressed woman having to visit a backstreet abortionist because of new, stricter limits on termination. But if you've spent four years obsessed with having a baby, the horror of a seedy illegal abortionist seems bearable in comparison to the tragedy of not conceiving. Sisters are important, but babies always come first.

Infertile couples are making abortion an issue once again. Even without becoming activists they are reopening a debate that their parents thought finished. The climate of opinion has changed so much that 42% of Britons today would like the abortion law to be tightened from 24 to 22 weeks. You can't ignore them: they're probably your neighbours.

■ Cristina Odone was editor of the *Catholic Herald* and deputy editor of the *New Statesman*.
29 March 2006

Can a foetus feel pain?

Information from the University of Birmingham

The idea that a foetus can feel pain is not supported by evidence according to a new clinical review published in the *British Medical Journal*.

In a paper which assesses current psychological and biological research on foetal pain, Dr Stuart Derbyshire from the University of Birmingham, School of Psychology argues that although foetuses are capable of producing a biological response to a pain stimulus, this does not mean they feel pain.

The paper concludes that the basic physical mechanisms we need to feel pain develop in a foetus from about the 26th week of pregnancy. Peripheral free nerve endings, which act as sensors for pain, reach full maturity between 23 and 25 weeks, and form a complete link with the thalamus and cortex by about 26 weeks. Around the same stage the thalamus and cortex develop important features of maturity.

The article argues that this biological response to a noxious or potentially dangerous stimulus, which is produced by almost all animals, is not sufficient for the experience of pain.

Dr Derbyshire explains: 'Experiencing pain is more than simply producing a biological response to a stimulus. It is something that comes from our experiences and develops due to stimulation and human interaction. Pain involves concepts such as location, feelings of unpleasantness and having the sensation of pain. Pain becomes possible because of a psychological development that begins at birth when the baby is separated from the protected atmosphere of the womb and is stimulated into wakeful activity.'

In the United States there have been a number of legal challenges to try to force all doctors to provide pain-killing injections to a foetus before an abortion is carried out.

Dr Derbyshire continues: 'The issue of foetal pain has become central to the ongoing battles about abortion in the US. However, the absence of foetal pain does not resolve the morality of abortion, but it does provide a strong argument against legal efforts to provide pain-killing injections for the foetus during the procedure.'

The paper 'Can Foetuses Feel Pain' is published in the *British Medical Journal* (BMJ Volume 332). *14 April 2006*

■ The above information is reprinted with kind permission from the University of Birmingham. Visit www.bham.ac.uk for more.
© *University of Birmingham 2006*

Foetal development

Information from Education For Choice

Pregnancy development

It is likely that many eggs that are fertilised do not successfully implant in the womb, but are discarded along with other dead tissue cells. For this reason the legal definition of pregnancy in the UK is when a fertilised cell is implanted in the womb.

Many implanted eggs spontaneously abort, causing what is commonly known as miscarriage. This can take place at any point in pregnancy, but is most common in the first 12 weeks. Some miscarriages take place so early in pregnancy that the woman is not aware of her pregnancy yet.

The 'primitive streak' is a term used to describe specific physical changes in the zygote that can be distinguished at about 14 days into pregnancy. After this time it is considered an embryo and UK law prohibits its use in experiments.

At the moment, 90% of abortions in Britain are carried out before 13 weeks, but abortion is still available legally up to 24 weeks. In very specific cases abortion can be provided after 24 weeks.

■ The above information is reprinted with kind permission from Education For Choice. Visit www.efc.org.uk for more information.
© *Education For Choice*

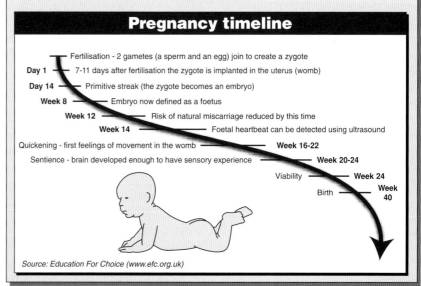

Pregnancy timeline

- Fertilisation - 2 gametes (a sperm and an egg) join to create a zygote
- **Day 1** — 7-11 days after fertilisation the zygote is implanted in the uterus (womb)
- **Day 14** — Primitive streak (the zygote becomes an embryo)
- **Week 8** — Embryo now defined as a foetus
- **Week 12** — Risk of natural miscarriage reduced by this time
- **Week 14** — Foetal heartbeat can be detected using ultrasound
- Quickening - first feelings of movement in the womb — **Week 16-22**
- Sentience - brain developed enough to have sensory experience — **Week 20-24**
- Viability — **Week 24**
- Birth — **Week 40**

Source: Education For Choice (www.efc.org.uk)

Viability

Information from Education For Choice

What is viability?

Viability means the capacity of a foetus to survive outside the woman's womb. Many people feel that viability is a morally significant point in pregnancy.

Viability is a contentious term, because there is no universally agreed definition of the term. These are some of the possible interpretations of the term.

- The lowest gestational age at which all newborn babies could survive.
- The lowest gestational age at which most newborn babies could survive.
- The lowest gestational age at which some or any newborn babies could survive.
- The lowest gestational age at which newborn babies could survive without any medical intervention.
- The lowest gestational age at which newborn babies could survive without long-term medical intervention.
- The lowest gestational age at which newborn babies could survive with ongoing or long-term medical intervention.
- The lowest gestational age at which newborn babies could survive without the likelihood of ongoing health or developmental problems.

Viability in the UK

In 1990 the time limit for most abortions was reduced from 28 to 24 weeks in order to take account of the increasing ability of medical staff to keep premature babies alive.

At 24 weeks many newborn babies in the UK will survive – some in good health, some with developmental problems, some with the need for long-term support and treatment. Some babies have been kept alive earlier even than this.

The skill of medics and the development of new technology are likely to increase the survival rate of babies born prematurely. However, the physiology of the developing foetus means that it is unlikely that the lower age limit for survival will fall much further.

Viability around the world

The likelihood of keeping a premature baby alive varies enormously depending on the health care services available in the region, country or continent. A very premature baby in a rural area within the developing world is unlikely to survive.

Therefore viability in one place means something quite different from viability in another.

Argument for the moral significance of viability

Many people consider that viability is the moment at which abortion becomes unacceptable. Up to the point of viability the survival of the foetus is inextricably linked to the woman and many people believe that as long as it is entirely dependent on the woman's body it cannot be said to be a person with independent rights.

After viability a foetus might survive inside or outside of the woman's body so it is less likely to be perceived as a part or an extension of the woman's body and more likely to be seen as a separate entity with separate rights.

Argument against the moral significance of viability

Many other arguments for and against the right of a woman to choose abortion do not rely on the issue of viability. For those who believe that the most important issue is the sanctity of life, and that all life is sacred from the moment of conception, the ongoing development of the foetus or its viability are not relevant.

For those who believe that a decision about abortion should be based on the circumstances a woman is in and her ability to care for and love a baby, the issue of viability is not relevant.

For those whose primary concern is the right of the woman to make a decision concerning her body and her life, viability might not be relevant.

The most morally problematic aspect of using viability as an absolute moral marker is that if the foetus is considered to have increased rights at viability, most foetuses in the developing world gain those rights long after most foetuses in the developed world. Taken to its logical conclusion, a foetus of 24 weeks in the developing world might have no moral or legal rights; whereas a foetus in the developed world would have a legal or moral right to life.

- The above information is reprinted with kind permission from Education For Choice. Visit www.efc.org.uk for more information.

© Education For Choice

Abortion and confidentiality

A research study published ahead of the Sue Axon judicial review shows that the vast majority of under-16s do confide in parents when considering abortion. Marie Stopes International warns: a change in current guidelines will place the most vulnerable girls at greater physical and emotional risk

A new research study, published today by Marie Stopes International, strongly endorses existing Department of Health guidelines guaranteeing confidential abortion services to under-16s. The guidelines are currently the subject of a judicial review process initiated by Sue Axon, the mother of two teenage daughters, who wants health professionals to be compelled to inform the parents of under-16s seeking abortion. A decision by Mr Justice Silbert in the High Court is expected shortly.

Marie Stopes International surveyed over 100 girls under the age of 16 attending for termination of pregnancy services at eight centres across England. Key findings include the following.

- More than seven out of 10 respondents (71%) had informed their mother and/or father of their intention to seek abortion. A further 8% had told another parental figure, such as their boyfriend's mother or an aunt.
- Almost one-quarter (23%) had told a teacher or school nurse.
- Only one respondent reported telling no one other than health professionals.
- Over nine out of 10 respondents (94%) were accompanied to the centre on the day they completed the questionnaire.
- Respondents who did not inform their parents reported a variety of reasons. The most common reason cited for not telling a mother was that they did not want to disappoint her. Frequently cited reasons for not telling fathers were: being afraid of an angry reaction; that they did not live with him; and not wishing to disappoint him.
- Almost seven out of 10 respondents (68%) did not support a change in the guidelines that would remove their right to confidential services.

'Clearly, for most girls, the question of confidentiality is not an issue because they readily confide in one or both of their parents,' said Liz Davies, Director of UK Operations for Marie Stopes International. 'The guidelines are not in place for those who have enough certainty in their relationship with their parents to take them into their confidence. They exist to protect the minority who, for whatever reason – real or imagined – do not feel such certainty.'

> *Over seven out of 10 respondents (71%) had informed their mother and/or father of their intention to seek abortion*

'In common with most other health professionals experienced in working with under-16s, Marie Stopes International feels that any alteration in the current guidelines would increase the hardship and emotional stress faced by vulnerable girls with unintended pregnancies and could deter them from seeking support and assistance from health providers, for fear that their confidence might be betrayed.

'In extreme circumstances, this could lead to concealed pregnancies and even attempts to self-abort, both of which could have severe physical and psychological consequences for the girls concerned. A rise in later terminations and sexually-transmitted infections (STIs) would also inevitably result as young people will simply not seek advice and services if they fear that their confidentiality will be compromised.'

The survey also showed that where under-16s did inform a parent, most received a positive reaction, both to the news of the pregnancy (with 51% of mothers being cited as being 'supportive') and to the decision to terminate (with 83% of mothers supporting this choice).

'Our hope is that more girls who find themselves in this situation and are unsure about telling their parents will be reassured by this finding,' added Ms Davies.

'It's really no surprise to find that parents, by and large, will react with love, compassion and support for their children in such circumstances. But sadly, there are always exceptions – and it is precisely to protect those who do not have a trusting and supportive relationship with their parents that these guidelines are in place.

'This research shows that what is needed is not a change in the guidance covering confidentiality, but rather increased efforts to provide teachers, school nurses and health staff providing adolescent services with the knowledge and skills to appropriately manage and support any under-16-year-old who, for whatever reason, cannot confide in a parent.

'It would be a complete betrayal of the most vulnerable young people in our society to change the existing guidance, so we are confident that the judicial review will conclude that the current guidelines should remain as they are.'
15 January 2006

- The above information is reprinted with kind permission from Marie Stopes International UK. Visit www.mariestopes.org.uk for more.

Rights and wrongs of teenage abortion

By Anne Karpf

It looked as if we were squaring up for a very old fight when, last year, Sue Axon first challenged the Department of Health's guidelines that allow under-16-year-olds to be given confidential advice about sexual matters. In the left corner the liberals, defending confidentiality as essential to avoid thousands more unwanted pregnancies. In the right corner the conservatives, claiming their parental rights were being usurped by professionals. For me it seemed like no contest: I hadn't marched for the liberalisation of abortion so many times only to have it whisked away from the most vulnerable all these years later. Now that Axon has lost, I still cleave to the same position and yet some of the glib certainties have ebbed away. Perhaps it's just a sign of middle-age to see beyond the slogans: today I subscribe less to 'free abortion on demand' than 'life's a bitch'.

Axon was easily vilified. Cast from the Victoria Gillick mould, she's one of those women who fleetingly becomes the darling of the New Right while appropriating the language of feminism: in place of 'a woman's right to choose' Axon defended the parent's 'right to know'. Some of her arguments were specious – contraception doesn't increase the likelihood of underage sex and abortion – but she highlighted the contradictions around parents' rights and responsibilities.

A child truants? Hold the parents responsible. Eats rubbish food and becomes obese? Again, blame the parents. Each time a new youth misdemeanour appears, the government proposes fining/re-educating/naming and shaming parents, while increasingly wary schools seek parental consent before they administer even aspirin. But, although you wouldn't countenance a teenager saying 'I'm going to go ahead and have my tonsils removed – it's got nothing to do with you',

when an adolescent gets pregnant and seeks an abortion, suddenly parents can be factored out.

I'm all for respecting teenagers' privacy yet I'd feel devastated if I read in my daughter's diary (which I don't – except that if it were open, with large print, I might), as one woman did, 'Had my termination (killed my baby)'. I could squeeze years of self-reproach from the knowledge that she'd gone through an experience like this without my support. Axon blames the state; I'd blame myself. Yet when I asked my 16-year-old whether, if she got pregnant, she'd discuss it with me, she replied, 'I'd definitely tell someone, but I don't know if it would be you.' I'd be supportive, she was sure, but she'd feel embarrassed and ashamed.

And here's where I find myself at odds with myself. Of course you can't legislate for family honesty, yet it's too sweeping to suggest that if an adolescent feels they can't be frank with their mother then their relationship must be lousy. Most teenagers go through periods when they're barely on speaking terms with their parents. Shouldn't we be glad that today they've got many sources of information and support, such as friends, magazines, websites? However right-on we feel we are or uninhibited we think parent-child discussion should be, many kids regard talking to their parents about sex as the apotheosis of embarrassment (as well as an unwelcome reminder that their parents have done it).

According to a recent Marie Stopes International survey, most girls who get pregnant do tell their mothers, but those who don't are motivated as much by the wish to protect them from worry as by the thought of a thundering paterfamilias. And anyway not all

parents, despite the family lobby's assumptions, are rational, calm, and loving.

In 2004, 3,756 girls under 15 had abortions, which I find shocking. Yet I'm increasingly riled by the view that abortion necessarily leaves behind a trail of depression and regret lasting years – to countless women of all ages whom I know it's only brought relief. Why is teenage pregnancy invariably seen as a disaster? And here's a heresy: if a girl has received sensitive counselling, should teenage abortion itself automatically be viewed as catastrophic?

Perhaps our problem is not really with pregnancy itself but with sex. Although ours is an over-sexualised society, adolescents have always fumbled their way through sexual initiation – this used to be seen as normal. The teenage girls I spoke to last week said things like 'Adults shouldn't worry so much,' and 'Teenage sex is made into such a big deal.' Instead of our perpetual angst, should we be following their lead and putting sex back into the corner where it belongs?

28 January 2006

© *Guardian Newspapers Limited 2006*

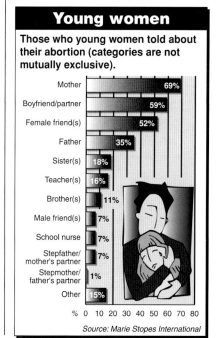

Young women

Those who young women told about their abortion (categories are not mutually exclusive).

Category	%
Mother	69%
Boyfriend/partner	59%
Female friend(s)	52%
Father	35%
Sister(s)	18%
Teacher(s)	16%
Brother(s)	11%
Male friend(s)	7%
School nurse	7%
Stepfather/mother's partner	7%
Stepmother/father's partner	1%
Other	15%

% 0 10 20 30 40 50 60 70 80

Source: Marie Stopes International

Teenage conceptions

Statistics and trends

Teenage conceptions

Under 20s: In 2004[a], 60.3 in every 1,000 15 to 19-year-olds became pregnant in England and Wales.[1] In Scotland, in 2003-2004,[a] the rate per 1,000 16 to 19-year-olds was 68.22.

Under 16s: In 2004, 7.5 in every 1,000 13 to 15-year-olds became pregnant in England and Wales.[1] In Scotland, in 2003-2004, the rate for the same age group was 7.52.

Outcome of teenage pregnancy

Abortions: The likelihood of a pregnant teenager having an abortion decreases with age. 61% of 14-year-olds have abortions; among 15-year-olds the figure is 55%, at 17, 41% and at 19, 35%.[3] (England & Wales 2003).

Births: In 2003[a] around 58,900 15 to 19-year-olds gave birth in England and Wales – a rate of 35.7 per 1,000.[1] In Northern Ireland in 2003, the number of teenage mothers was 1,484[4] – a rate of 22.9 per 1,000[b].

In Scotland, 4,984 16 to 19-year-olds gave birth in 2003 – a rate of 39.4 per 1,000[2].

Teenage pregnancy – is the trend up or down?

Teenagers are far less likely to get pregnant today than they were in the early 1970s. The conception rate in 1970 was 82.4 per 1,000 15 to 19-year-olds compared with 59.8 in 2003[c].

The decline in teenage mothers is even more striking. In 1970, 71.4 per 1,000 15 to 19-year-olds had a baby, almost twice the rate in 2003. The proportion of pregnant teenagers choosing motherhood declined sharply after the 1967 Abortion Act offered young people the choice of terminating an unwanted pregnancy.

Teenage pregnancy – the trends over the last 25 years

After the introduction of free contraception on the NHS in 1974, teenage conception rates for the 15

to 19 age group steadily declined, reaching the lowest recorded figure in 1983.

Later in the 1980s that downward trend reversed. Between 1983 and 1990 the rate rose by 23%. Rates fell again in the early 1990s but rose between 1995 and 1998. Since 1998 the teenage conception rate has started to decline, falling overall by 7% to 2004.

The conception rate for 13 to 15-year-olds has followed much the same pattern as for older teenagers, but usually with less marked variation. Since 1998, however, the conception rate for under 16s has fallen by 17%.

Between 1998 and 2004 there was also a fall of 11% in conception rates amongst under-18s from 47.1 per thousand to 41.7 per thousand.[1]

What caused the teenage conception rate to rise in the 1980s?

Fears over confidentiality: research has shown consistently that young people will not use services unless they are sure that they are confidential. It is Brook's experience that controversy in the 1980s around the question of providing contraception confidentially to under-16s confused many of their clients over the right to advice and may have deterred many young people from visiting contraceptive services. Attendance figures for under-16s at Brook and family planning clinics in England showed a significant drop during this period. Although the legal issues surrounding confidentiality and under-16s were resolved in the House of Lords in 1985 in favour of young people's rights, attendance figures for this age group did not recover until 1990.[5]

Cuts in services: funding cuts in community health services forced the closure of many family planning and young people's services, restricting access to help.

Unemployment and youth opportunities: the effect of the recession increased youth unemployment, undermining young people's motivation to delay having a baby.

...and fall in the 1990s?

In England and Wales, between 1990 and 1995, there was a 15% reduction in the conception rate among 15 to 19-year-olds and a 16% decline amongst under-16s. This coincided with an expansion of young people's services from 52% of health authorities providing a specialist service in 1990 to over 85% in 1995. This downward trend was reversed in 1996.

The impact of the 1995 pill alert

In 1996, teenage conception rates in England and Wales rose significantly. This followed the pill alert in 1995 about the apparent increased risk of venous thromboembolism in 'third generation' pills. The percentage of Brook clients choosing the pill in 1996 dropped by 32% among the under-16s and 25% among 16 to 19-year-olds.[6]

Making progress

In the late 1990s teenage conception rates resumed their downward trend. Strategies to reduce teenage pregnancy and improve sexual health have been developed for all parts of the UK. In England the number of services for young people has continued to increase. The number of sessions at birth control services especially for people under 20 tripled between 1994-1995 and 2003-2004, as did the number of young women attending them. In Wales the number of women under 20 attending clinics almost doubled between 1993-1994 and 2003-2004.

Factors associated with teenage parenthood [7]

Low educational attainment: low educational attainment is the most powerful single factor associated with becoming a young parent.

Poverty: teenage parents are more likely to come from families with low socio-economic status and financial hardship.

Emotional difficulties: Young parents, particularly teenage mothers, are much more likely to have a history of serious behaviour problems.

Being a child of a teenage mother: 26% of young mothers and 22% of young fathers had teenage mothers compared with 13% of women and men who became parents at a later age.

Regional variations in teenage pregnancy rates

Teenage conception rates vary widely across the country. In 2003, South East London Health Authority had a conception rate of 90.7 per thousand 15 to 19-year-olds, compared with a rate of 44.8 in Surrey and Sussex.[3]

The teenage conception rate is considerably higher in deprived areas of the country compared with affluent areas. However, pregnant teenagers in more affluent areas are more likely to choose abortion.[8]

Teenage mothers and single parents

Although teenagers are far less likely to have a baby today compared with 30 years ago, they are more likely to have the baby outside marriage. This reflects the trend away from the 'shotgun marriage' which carried a high risk of divorce, towards cohabitation. In 2003 73% of babies born to teenage women outside marriage in England and Wales were jointly registered by both parents and 54% of parents were resident at the same address.[9]

26% of young mothers and 22% of young fathers had teenage mothers

---

However, teenagers make up only a small proportion of single parents. The proportion of births outside marriage born to teenagers decreased from 35% to 15% between 1972 to 2004.[9]

International comparisons

Factors associated with low teenage pregnancy rates:[10]
- an open and accepting attitude to teenage sexuality;
- widely available information and sex education;
- easy access to confidential contraceptive services.

The Netherlands has the lowest teenage conception rate of developed countries – one-sixth of that in the United Kingdom. Comparable conception data is not available from other European countries. However, in an international comparison of teenage birth rates, the United Kingdom topped the European league.[11]

Footnotes

a   Latest available figures.

b   Conception data is not collected in Northern Ireland because no abortions are recorded. The only available statistics are for teenage births.

c   England and Wales only. Comparable data over the same period of time is not available for Scotland or Northern Ireland.

References

1. Conceptions in England and Wales, 2004. *Health Statistics Quarterly* 29. National Statistics Spring 2006.
2. Information and Statistics Division Website, Scottish Health Service. Provisional figures.
3. Conceptions in England and Wales 2003. *Health Statistics Quarterly* 26, Summer 2005, National Statistics 2005.
4. Northern Ireland Registrar General's *Annual Report 2003*.
5. *NHS Contraceptive Services, England: 1997 to 1998*. Department of Health.
6. Brook Advisory Centres *Annual Report 1996 to 1997*.
7. Social Backgrounds and Post-birth Experiences of Young Parents. Joseph Rowntree Foundation. *Social Policy Research* 80. July 1995.
8. Influence of socio-economic factors on attaining targets. T Smith, *British Medical Journal*, 306, 1993.
9. *Birth Statistics: Report of the Registrar General on Births and Patterns of Family Building in England and Wales, 2004*. Series FM1, no. 33. National Statistics.
10. Teenage Pregnancy in Developed Countries: Determinants and policy implications. E Jones et al. *Family Planning Perspectives*, Vol 17, Mar/Apr 1995.
11. *A League Table of Teenage Births in Rich Nations*, United Nations Children's Fund Innocenti Research Centre, 2001.

March 2006

- The above information is reprinted with kind permission from Brook. Brook provides free and confidential sexual health advice and services specifically for young people under 25. For further information, visit www.brook.org.uk or contact the Young People's Information Service by calling 0800 0185 023 or texting BROOK HELP to 81222.

© Brook Advisory Centre

DIY abortions

Women to get go-ahead for DIY abortions in their home

DIY abortions for women in their own homes will be given the go-ahead, it emerged yesterday.

Under the scheme, mothers-to-be will be allowed to take a series of powerful tablets that trigger a miscarriage at home instead of in hospital.

But many believe the Department of Health plan to allow 'bedroom abortions' could lead to women suffering life-threatening complications.

It is feared abortion rates will rise, with young girls finding the prospect of a quick-fix termination appealing.

Women anxious to hide their pregnancy may also prefer the 'secrecy' of having their abortion at home, rather than in a hospital.

Almost 200,000 abortions are carried out each year in the UK. About 25,000 'medical abortions' using pills are carried out on women under nine weeks pregnant each year.

At the moment, a woman goes to a hospital or clinic to take a pill, which blocks vital pregnancy hormones and causes the foetus to detach from the womb lining.

She returns 48 hours later for a second tablet. Contractions, which may be very painful, are followed by an enforced 'miscarriage', which can take up to six to eight hours. Doctors then check the patient to ensure the process is complete.

Under the proposals, women will make just one visit to hospital. They would be given one pill to take immediately and a second to take at home two days later. They would be advised to have a check-up 14 days after that.

Those in favour of the method say it gives women more control and allows the most traumatic part of the procedure to take part in familiar surroundings.

One of two trials being run by the Department of Health has already

By Fiona MacRae, Science Reporter

been declared a success. The *Nursing Standard* magazine said 172 women had safely taken the pills.

They were not treated in a hospital, but did have a nurse at their side.

Project manager Shirley Butler told the magazine: 'This has been a successful pilot and it has proved that abortion is safe outside a hospital. We have had a few problems. Some women experienced pain and they were given painkillers.

'One woman had haemorrhaging, but if she had been at home she would have called our helpline and she would have been given help.' The British Pregnancy Advisory Service, the country's biggest provider of abortions, has been campaigning for several years for women to be able to take the second pill at home.

But pro-life campaigners have condemned the plans as a cost-cutting exercise and a step back to the days of backstreet abortions.

Using the pills removes the need for anaesthetists, operating theatre staff and surgeons.

But fears have been raised about the drug's safety. Figures from the UK Medicines and Healthcare Products Regulatory Agency show three British women have died after using the abortion pill since 1991. A further 79 have had suspected adverse reactions to it.

In the US, where 100,000 women a year take mifepristone, or RU-486 – the pills also used in Britain – five women have died and 607 have suffered serious complications.

Home abortions are available in the US and France.

Critics attacked the plans, saying women's health was being put at risk.

Josephine Quintavalle, of Comment on Reproductive Ethics, said:

'There is no such thing as a good abortion but I can't think of a worse way to do it than this.

'It is a way of doing it without people occupying hospital space. But it doesn't take much to imagine the process of being at home on your own and going to the bathroom and seeing what's actually happening and seeing the loss of a child is going to be very traumatic.

'There is a sense that this will be an option for young girls trying to keep things hidden. It may be easier to take a pill at home and hope Mum doesn't find out.'

Nuala Scarisbrick, of campaigning group LIFE, said: 'I cannot think of anything worse than having to abort at home, with the sudden bleeding, stomach cramps, nausea and fainting it can involve.

'The woman could be all on her own. She may not have told anyone about her pregnancy.

'If she is found bleeding heavily in the bathroom, no one will know what has gone wrong.'

The Health Department said trials of medical abortion outside hospitals are continuing.

A spokesman said no changes to the way abortions are carried out will be approved unless the Department is content that there is no risk to the woman's safety and the type of place where abortions take place has been determined.

■ This article first appeared in the *Daily Mail*, 16 February 2006.

© 2006 Associated Newspapers Ltd

What's wrong with 'do-it-yourself' abortions?

Information from the Pro-Choice Forum

The British press always gets itself in a tangle over abortion, largely because it tries to follow public opinion and public opinion is muddled. Nobody likes the idea of abortion but most people think it is necessary – 'the least worse option' for a woman with an unwanted pregnancy. Most people want abortion to be provided safely and legally and preferably as early in pregnancy as possible.

Typical media muddle-headedness was expressed in *The Times* (London) last week. In response to news that the number of women using the abortion pill was rising rapidly, a *Times* leader column on 29 May argued that 'the popularity of early medical abortion should prompt soul-searching.'

The risks of early medical abortion are extremely small and considerably less than the risks of pregnancy

The news that in 2005 the number of women using the abortion pill at British Pregnancy Advisory Service clinics had doubled to 10,000, and that the charity, which provides a quarter of all British abortions, was seeing 65 per cent of clients in the first nine weeks of pregnancy – up from 56 per cent the year before – could and should have been an unequivocally 'good news story'.

Early medical abortion – or EMA – is when a woman takes a pill that results in the ending of her pregnancy. It is recommended by medical organisations as the best way to end a pregnancy in its earliest weeks. It avoids any surgical

By Ann Furedi, chief executive, BPAS

intervention, which reduces the risk of complications, especially infection. It is also cost effective for the National Health Service because it doesn't involve the use of theatres, gynaecologists or anaesthetists. The woman attends her clinic to be provided with the necessary medication and then returns home where she loses the pregnancy, much as she would do if she were to have a spontaneous miscarriage.

The use of early medical abortion also allows women to access services more quickly. Doctors are sometimes reluctant to carry out surgical abortions at very early gestations, because it is more difficult for them to be sure they have completed the procedure – but with early medical abortion, earlier is always better. And this in itself makes it preferable for many women. Today's pregnancy tests can confirm a pregnancy even

before a woman has missed her period, and most women wanting abortion care want it as soon as possible. Preferably yesterday.

Improving access to early abortion is central to the UK government's sexual health strategy. Local Primary Care Trusts (PCTs) have been given additional funding to help them achieve targets for the number of abortions that are carried out before 10 weeks of pregnancy, and access to the abortion pill is widely understood to be a means to achieve this. The Department of Health has specifically advised PCTs that they should ensure women have the option of the abortion pill.

So why the soul-searching? *The Times* leader said: 'The rise in EMA's popularity may be explicable; it is not necessarily to be welcomed. Parliament has repeatedly reaffirmed a woman's right to choose. Such a choice must never be easy.' Why not? *The Times* also said that the abortion pill has many critics who say that EMA 'could give rise to a false

---

Abortions after 16 weeks

Percentage of women seeking abortion after 16 weeks by reason given.

Reason	Percentage
Woman did not realise she was pregnant	71%
Difficulty making abortion arrangements	48%
Afraid to tell parents or partner	33%
Needed time to make decision	24%
Hoped relationship would change	8%
Pressure not to have abortion	8%
Something changed during pregnancy	6%
Didn't know timing was important	6%
Didn't know she could get an abortion	5%
Foetal abnormality diagnosed late	2%
Other	11%

Source: Abortion time limits, British Medical Association. From Torres A, Forrest JD. Why do women have abortions? Fam Plann Perspect. 1988;20(4):169-176.

---

impression that an abortion even in the early stages of pregnancy is relatively simple without physical or psychological risk. This is not true.'

Well, actually it is – almost. Of course, no medical procedure is entirely risk-free, but the risks of early medical abortion are extremely small and considerably less than the risks of pregnancy. And studies have shown repeatedly that early abortion of an unwanted pregnancy does not put women at risk of psychological damage. The 'many critics' who disturb journalists so much are not just concerned about the abortion pill but about abortion in principle. They are horrified by the existence of a drug that makes the experience of abortion easier for women.

It is understandable that if you believe the destruction of foetal life is evil, you will oppose the use of a pill that allows this to be achieved more easily

---

The critics are entitled to their views. It is understandable that if you believe the destruction of foetal life is evil, you will oppose the use of a pill that allows this to be achieved more easily. That is honest opposition. What is dishonest, however, is to brief journalists that women can't cope with the experience, or that women's health is harmed. It is fair enough to say the abortion pill is wrong, if you believe that; it is intolerable to claim that it is unsafe.

Medical abortion is not new. Women have tried to use herbs and medicines for abortion for as long as they have wanted to end pregnancies. Evidence that women used abortifacient herbs dates back to the Egyptians. In the past, though, the success of the methods were somewhat hit and miss; usually more miss. Beecham's remedies never have been an effective way to interrupt a pregnancy; other more traditional folk remedies, such as ergomot, may

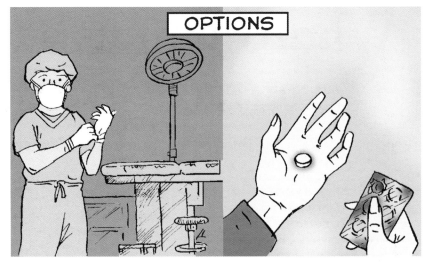

OPTIONS

have achieved the desired result sometimes, for some women. Today, however, women can legally access a safe, reliable, effective method of medical abortion. The latest figures show that they are doing so in ever-growing numbers.

No woman ever wants to have an abortion. It is the solution to a problem they wish they didn't have. Most women struggle with their decision to end a pregnancy. The availability of the abortion pill does not make their decision easier. It may, however, make the process easier. And why should that be wrong?
5 June 2006

■ The above information is reprinted with kind permission from the Pro-Choice Forum. Visit www.prochoiceforum.org.uk for more information.

© *Pro-Choice Forum*

UK aborts over 20 babies for minor disabilities

Information from LIFE

The pro-life charity LIFE reacted with dismay to news that more than 20 babies have been aborted in advanced pregnancy because scans showed that they had club feet or webbed fingers or extra digits.

Michaela Aston, a spokeswoman for LIFE, said: 'What sort of society tolerates the abortion of unborn children simply because of club feet, cleft palate or webbed fingers?'

'One sympathises for many of the parents of these unborn children aborted after disability has been detected. What information are they being given by health care professionals so that they can make a truly informed choice? We suspect that many parents make the decision to opt for abortion in complete ignorance of the help and support available to children with disabilities and their families. For this, health care professionals must shoulder a large part of the blame.'

'Surely Parliament can no longer sit back and do nothing whilst the Abortion Act is so blatantly abused? If, as a society, we are truly committed to equality for people with disabilities then such blatant discrimination against the disabled unborn must stop.'
28 May 2006

■ The above information is reprinted with kind permission from LIFE. Visit www.lifeuk.org for more information.

© *LIFE*

Abortion and disability

Young people's attitudes to abortion for foetal abnormality: report of the findings of a study looking at school and university students' opinions

Summary of findings

- The vast majority of students believe that abortion should be legal, and dislike the idea of the law dictating the course of action for the pregnant woman.
- School students were often more extreme in their views than university students, which can perhaps be attributed to their lack of experience and knowledge.

Concern was expressed that abortion for abnormality could be, or at least could encourage, discrimination against disabled people

---

- The terms 'pro-choice' and 'pro-life' do not imply a consistent support for or opposition to abortion. A significant number of 'pro-life' students support abortion in some cases, and some 'pro-choice' students believe there should be some limits placed on the right to choose.
- Where students think there should be a limit on the right to choose, they suggest the need

pro+choice forum

for more education, counselling or a change in people's attitudes to bring this about, rather than legal measures.

- Abortion for foetal abnormality was thought by most students to be understandable in some cases, although most thought it would be wrong to have an abortion purely because the child was disabled.
- Many students believed that the decision to abort an abnormal foetus should be based around the welfare of the child, and the quality of life a child will have. Abortion where the parents simply did not want a disabled child was often labelled 'selfish'.
- Students often suggested that disability could have positive as well as negative aspects and that people should value the special talents and caring nature that disabled people, particularly Down's syndrome children, were thought to have.

- Students perceived disability to be an attribute or form of identity, akin to gender or skin colour, rather than as a disease or illness. Since the issue of disability was therefore thought of as a rights rather than a health issue, concern was expressed that abortion for abnormality could be, or at least could encourage, discrimination against disabled people.
- There was a dislike expressed of 'consumerism' and 'too much choice'. Some students thought that people can expect to be able to have anything they want, including a 'perfect child', which was seen as morally wrong.
- Students expressed fear about the so-called 'slippery slope' where they thought abortion for abnormality could lead to sex selection, or abortion on the grounds of hair and eye colour.
- Students expressed fears about the consequences of genetic manipulation on the grounds that it is 'against nature' and may spin out of control.

- The above information is reprinted with kind permission from the Pro-Choice Forum. Visit www.prochoiceforum.org.uk for more.

© Pro-Choice Forum

Women demand tougher laws to curb abortions

- **Poll reveals growing concern over late terminations**
- **Blair under pressure to agree review as MPs urge change**

By Denis Campbell and Gaby Hinsliff

A majority of women in Britain want the abortion laws to be tightened to make it harder, or impossible, for them to terminate a pregnancy.

Evidence of a widespread public demand for the government to further restrict women's right to have an abortion is revealed in a remarkable *Observer* opinion poll. The findings have reignited the highly-charged debate on abortion, and increased the pressure on Tony Blair to review the current time limits.

The survey by MORI shows that 47 per cent of women believe the legal limit for an abortion should be cut from its present 24 weeks, and another 10 per cent want the practice outlawed altogether. Among the population overall, reducing the upper limit was the preferred option backed by the largest proportion of respondents, 42 per cent, made up of a 36 to 47 per cent split among men and women.

Only one person in three agreed that 'the current time limit is about right', with slightly fewer women (31 per cent) than men (35 per cent) saying that. Just 2 per cent of women and 5 per cent of men think the last possible date after which a woman can end a pregnancy should be increased from 24 weeks.

The leader of the 4.1 million Catholics in England and Wales, Cardinal Cormac Murphy O'Connor, called on politicians last night to heed the evidence of a growing demand for a rethink on abortion policy, to include the *Observer's* findings. 'There has been a moral awakening over the last few years about abortion; the British public have been undergoing a reality check,' said his spokesman, Dr Austen Ivereigh. 'The Cardinal sees in this moral awakening a growing unease with, and erosion of, the idea of abortion as simply a woman's right.'

Increased awareness of the realities of abortion, and the impact of ultrasound images of a 23-week-old foetus smiling and grimacing, have made people change their views, said Ivereigh. The latter 'very dramatically showed that what had been depersonalised in many people's minds as a foetus was clearly seen to be a baby, a human being in formation, and that has come as a shock to many people', he added.

Abortion became a key issue in last year's general election campaign when Michael Howard, then the Conservative leader, said he wanted to see the maximum time limit cut to 20 weeks.

Former Liberal leader David Steel, the architect of the pioneering 1967 Abortion Act which made abortions legal for the first time in Britain, wants the upper limit reduced to 22 weeks.

The limit was originally set in 1967 at 28 weeks, because that was then taken to be the age at which a foetus would not be 'viable', but it was reduced to 24 weeks in 1990. Around 200,000 women a year undergo an abortion in Britain, although between 85 and 90 per cent occur within 12 weeks and only about 1.5 per cent after 20 weeks. Abortion is still illegal in Northern Ireland.

David Cameron, Howard's successor, backs a new limit of between 20 and 22 weeks. 'He thinks because of the advances in medical science there's now a case for it being lowered, although not dramatically. He would support it being reduced. That is his personal view,' said his spokesman.

Moves to reduce the time limit are now beginning to win the support of liberal-minded MPs who support the right to abortion. Dr Evan Harris, the Liberal Democrat MP and a former GP, called for an in-depth parliamentary inquiry to examine the scientific evidence about the survival rates of babies born at under 24 weeks, and then recommend any necessary changes

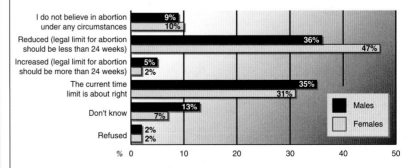

Abortion time limits

Respondents were asked 'The current legal time period for an abortion to take place is when a woman is up to 24 weeks pregnant. That is, women are allowed to have an abortion at any time within the first 24 weeks of her pregnancy. Do you believe that this time limit should be reduced, increased, or is it about right?'

	Males	Females
I do not believe in abortion under any circumstances	9%	10%
Reduced (legal limit for abortion should be less than 24 weeks)	36%	47%
Increased (legal limit for abortion should be more than 24 weeks)	5%	2%
The current time limit is about right	35%	31%
Don't know	13%	7%
Refused	2%	2%

Results are based on 1,790 British adults aged 15 to 64 years and data is weighted to reflect national population profile. Fieldwork conducted online between 6 and 10 Jan 2006. The base for males is 830; for females, 960.

Source: Ipsos MORI 2006.

to the law. 'The question has been raised about whether we are going to base the limit on viability – that was the basis under the existing law – and if it's on viability then viability is subject to change based on medical advances,' he said.

'The longer we don't debate this, the less confidence the public will have that Parliament is doing its job which is reviewing and keeping in mind how scientific advances impact on public policy.'

Abortion law has always been altered through private members' bills tabled by backbenchers rather than by government in the past, with MPs voting according to their conscience. However the tacit support of the government is vital to get private members' bills through, making the views of the prime minister and health secretary crucial.

Amid the debate last year, prompted by the images of unborn babies in the womb, Blair indicated that the government could be prepared to review the limits on abortion law. The then Health Secretary, John Reid, personally supports a lower time limit.

However, Patricia Hewitt, the current Health Secretary, seemed yesterday to rule out any reduction: 'I think it is very difficult for a woman contemplating a late termination and they need to be given very clear advice and support.'

Toni Belfield of the Family Planning Association, which opposes any reduction, said: 'The argument about medical advances misses the point. There needs to be access to late abortion after 20 weeks because a woman may not find out she is pregnant until 18 or 19 weeks, or be in a non-consensual relationship, or be told about a foetal abnormality.'

Julia Millington, of the Pro-Life Alliance of anti-abortion groups, said the findings were 'very encouraging'.

Ipsos MORI interviewed 1,790 people aged 16 to 64 by online questionnaire between 6 and 10 January.

29 January 2006

The 24-week limit

New research study examining women's experiences of late abortion underlines need to retain the current 24-week limit

A new research study which examines the reasoning, experiences and opinions of over 100 women who have recently undergone late abortion is published today by Marie Stopes International (MSI), the UK's leading provider of abortion services. MSI believes that this report presents a compelling case for retaining the current 24-week legal limit for abortion in the face of growing political, social and media pressure for a reduction.

Less than 2 per cent of all abortions taking place in England and Wales annually are carried out after 20 weeks' gestation, but MSI argues that a reduction in the limit would not reduce demand for later abortions, but merely increase the hardship and emotional suffering of women facing unplanned pregnancies who might be denied access if the law is changed.

Key findings from the study, which combined a series of face-to-face interviews and self-completed questionnaires of over 100 women terminating pregnancies between 19 and 24 weeks' gestation and was carried out in the first four months of 2005, include the following.

■ For the majority of women taking part, signs and symptoms of pregnancy were not recognised until an advanced stage, making late abortion an inevitability rather than a conscious choice on their part.

'I continued to have periods up 'til I was four months, not knowing I was pregnant.' (aged 27)

■ A minority of women were aware of their pregnancy early on, but were either in denial or subsequently faced a significant change in circumstances that forced them to re-evaluate their pregnancy.

'My partner is violent but when he found out I was pregnant he promised to get help... He then beat me with a baseball bat so I don't think it's right to involve a child in that.' (aged 24)

■ Most women thought long and hard about their decision, discussed it with people close to them and appreciated having time to consider their options.

'It's a very difficult decision to make. The extra time is often needed. Better that than an unwanted child.' (no age given)

■ Most women reported a combination of factors influencing their decision – every woman's situation was unique and most felt that they were the only person capable of making the decision.

'I never expected to find myself in this situation and now understand just how distressing it is and what a hard decision it is to make.' (aged 37)

■ Some women encountered delays accessing abortion services due to obstructive practitioners or administrative delays.

'The first doctor I went to, she was just not willing to listen to a reason, she didn't want to know why... At the end of the day, it's our choice, they should be more sympathetic.' (aged 35)

■ Women taking part in the study were clear about the strongly negative consequences on their lives, should they have been refused access to abortion at later gestations.

'I was getting low and I hated myself. And I wouldn't have thought twice about taking my own life.' (aged 23)

'In recent months it seems that everyone – from politicians and medical professionals to journalists and anti-abortion advocates – has been allowed to speak out on the issue of late abortion, except for those for whom it is most important; the women who have experienced it,' said Liz Davies, Marie Stopes International's Director of UK Operations.

'We feel that this study goes some way to redressing that oversight. What emerges very clearly from this research is that no woman who opted for late abortion made the decision lightly. To suggest otherwise is to do these women a great disservice.

'As a society we should be supporting women and respecting their right to choose what they consider to be in their own best interests and the interests of their existing families and their unborn child, not condemning them or calling for measures that would limit their options and cause real hardship.'

Ms Davies also welcomed the result of the recent British Medical Association debate on late abortion, where three out of every four doctors taking part voted to retain the current limit for abortion.

'Clearly the medical profession is strongly of the opinion that there is no case around foetal viability at 24 weeks or less to warrant a change to the current limit,' she said.

'We must recognise that there will always be a need for later terminations, as a proportion of women, through no fault of their own, either do not recognise symptoms of pregnancy or have no reason to suspect that they could possibly be pregnant at all if, for example, they are regularly using a modern form of contraception.

'We could, however, at least assist in reducing the gestation at which some women present for abortion if we worked to remove some of the barriers to access which can cause unreasonable delays in obtaining abortion services. A useful start would be the reform of the current legislation to remove the archaic requirement that women seek written permission from two doctors before any abortion may proceed and to compel doctors who hold a conscientious objection to abortion to immediately refer a woman on to someone who is willing to help her.'

A full copy of the report: *Late Abortion: A Research Study of Women Undergoing Abortion between 19 and 24 Weeks' Gestation* can be obtained by writing to press@mariestopes.org.uk or going to www.mariestopes.org.uk/uk/publications.htm.

15 July 2005

■ The above information is reprinted with kind permission from Marie Stopes International UK. Visit www.mariestopes.org.uk for more information.

Charity calls for Abortion Act review

Government must listen on abortion law review, says LIFE

LIFE, the national caring charity, has added its voice to the increasing demands for a review of the Abortion Act, following the release of the latest statistics on abortion. The rate of abortion remains extremely high, with almost 200,000 terminations carried out in 2005, but the government is refusing to allow such a review, despite calls by prominent parliamentarians and a growing recognition among the general public that it is time for a change.

67 MPs, including pro-abortion members such as Dr Evan Harris, have now signed a motion calling for a review of the Abortion Act. The House of Commons Science and Technology Committee has also recommended the setting up of a joint committee of the Commons and the Lords to review the law. This is long overdue, given the huge advances in medical technology that have occurred since the last review in 1990, and the huge strides that have been made in understanding unborn life. There is also a greater awareness of the humanity of the unborn child, thanks in large part to the 4-D ultrasound images pioneered by Professor Stuart Campbell.

LIFE spokeswoman Michaela Aston noted that the high rate of abortion demonstrates a clear and urgent demand for the kind of positive, professional caring services offered by LIFE. 'Recent poll data shows that 85% of British women believe that more resources need to be put into providing alternatives to abortion, with only 8% saying that abortion should be more easily accessible. The government should respond to this overwhelming demand by providing much more support to organisations such as LIFE. We provide practical help for women with unplanned pregnancies, promoting healthy, positive solutions which respect life and empower women.'

4 July 2006

■ The above information is reprinted with kind permission from LIFE, the national pro-life charity. Visit www.lifeuk.org for more information.

YouGov questioned 2,432 adults aged 18+ throughout Britain online between 19 and 24 August 2005 on the subjects of abortion, cloning and euthanasia.

At the moment abortion is legal in Britain up to the 24th week of pregnancy. However, doctors can now save the lives of premature babies born as early as 23 weeks. From what you know, what do you think the legal limit for abortions should be?

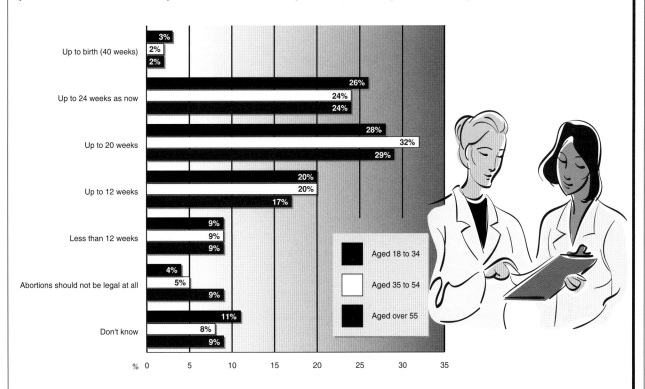

From what you know, do you think some women do not protect themselves adequately against unwanted pregnancies and instead use abortion as a means of birth control?

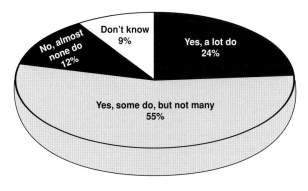

Do you, or do you not, believe that abortion should be free on demand on the NHS?

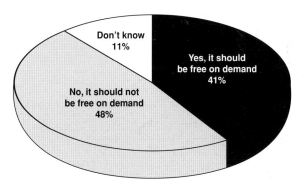

Apart from the question of what the exact legal limit should be, do you think it is too difficult or too easy for women to obtain abortions in Britain, or are the present arrangements broadly satisfactory?

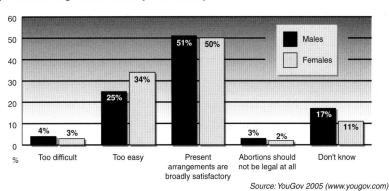

Source: YouGov 2005 (www.yougov.com)

- One in five pregnancies in the UK end in termination. (page 6)

- 90% of all abortions take place in the first 12 weeks of pregnancy. (page 6)

- Abortion in England and Wales was first made illegal in the 19th century. Before then English Common Law had allowed abortion provided it was carried out before the woman felt the foetus move ('quickening') when it was believed the soul entered the body. (page 7)

- Despite the availability of effective contraception, it is estimated that one in three babies is unplanned. (page 9)

- Between two and five per cent of babies conceived have a congenital abnormality. (page 9)

- 94% of legal abortions are carried out under ground C, which states that the continuance of the pregnancy would involve risk, greater than if the pregnancy were terminated, of injury to the physical or mental health of the pregnant woman. (page 10)

- Aborting an unwanted foetus during a woman's first pregnancy does not increase her risk of depression and may actually make her less likely to suffer the blues, a report says. (page 11)

- While some women might feel relieved after terminating a pregnancy, it's also very common to feel sad, guilty, even confused, especially if you felt that at another time a baby would have been right for you. (page 11)

- The Abortion Act 1967 says that two doctors must agree that an abortion would cause less damage to a woman's physical or mental health than continuing with the pregnancy. (page 12)

- Men have the right to avoid conceiving unplanned pregnancies either by choosing not to have sex or to use condoms: currently condoms are the only form of contraception over which a man can take full responsibility. Beyond this, men have few rights in a decision about their partner's pregnancy because the law makes no other provision. (page 15)

- In 2005, the latest full year for which statistics are available, 186,400 abortions took place in England and Wales. That's a rate of 17.8 per thousand women aged 15-44. (page 18)

- In 2005 the rate of abortions per thousand 15-19 year olds in England and Wales was 23 and in 20-24 year olds it was also 32. (page 18)

- In 2006 alone an estimated 19 million women will undergo an unsafe abortion. Nearly 70,000 of them will pay for it with their lives. (page 19)

- A survey showed that 62 per cent of 18 to 24 year olds said they did not have enough information about the risks of unprotected sex. (page 23)

- In Kingston and Richmond in London, only half of all abortions are NHS funded compared to 90 per cent in Coventry. In 2001, 79 per cent of women in North East Lincolnshire obtained an abortion before ten weeks compared to just 26 per cent in Great Yarmouth. (page 24)

- The idea that a foetus can feel pain is not supported by evidence according to a new clinical review published in the *British Medical Journal*. (page 26)

- It is likely that many eggs that are fertilised do not successfully implant in the womb, but are discarded along with other dead tissue cells. For this reason the legal definition of pregnancy in the UK is when a fertilised cell is implanted in the womb. (page 26)

- In 1990 the time limit for most abortions was reduced from 28 to 24 weeks in order to take account of the increasing ability of medical staff to keep premature babies alive. (page 27)

- Over seven out of 10 respondents to a survey of under-16s seeking abortion (71%) had informed their mother and/or father of their intention to seek abortion. A further eight percent had told another parental figure, such as their boyfriend's mother or an aunt. (page 28)

- The likelihood of a pregnant teenager having an abortion decreases with age. 61% of 14-year-olds have abortions; among 15-year-olds the figure is 55%, at 17, 41% and at 19, 35%. (page 30)

- A majority of women in Britain want the abortion laws to be tightened to make it harder, or impossible, for them to terminate a pregnancy. (page 36)

- 55% of people responding to a YouGov survey felt that some women used abortion as a form of contraception, but not many. (page 39)

- 34% of women felt that it was too easy to obtain an abortion in Britain, compared to 25% of men. Only 3% of women and 4% of men felt it was too difficult, while 50% of women and 51% of men felt the present arrangements for obtaining an abortion were broadly satisfactory. (page 39)

GLOSSARY

Abortion
Also called termination. The deliberate ending of an unwanted pregnancy by medical means. Abortion is a controversial issue in the UK and generates a lot of debate.

Conception
The moment at which a male sperm fertilises a female egg, resulting in pregnancy.

Contraception
Anything which prevents conception (pregnancy). The most common types are the so-called 'barrier methods' such as condoms, which work by stopping sperm from reaching an egg during intercourse, and hormonal methods such as the contraceptive pill, which change the way the female user's body works to prevent an egg from being fertilised, or in the case of emergency contraception (the 'morning-after pill'), to prevent a fertilised egg from becoming implanted in the womb. Some pro-life supporters believe that emergency contraception is a form of abortion, as it results in the termination of an already-fertilised egg.

Do-It-Yourself (DIY) abortions
A term coined to describe plans which will allow women to receive the drugs necessary for early medical abortion so that these can be taken in their own homes.

Early medical abortion
This type of abortion usually takes place in the first nine weeks of pregnancy. The pregnant woman is required to take two tablets, which cause the body to expel the pregnancy, much like a natural miscarriage.

Embryo
Between day 14 and week eight of pregnancy, the fertilised egg is referred to as an embryo.

Foetus
After the eighth week of pregnancy, an unborn baby is referred to as a foetus.

Gametes
Term used to describe a male sperm and female egg, which have the potential to unite to form a zygote.

Gestation
This refers to the carrying of an embryo or foetus inside the womb.

Global Gag Rule
Also known as the Mexico City Policy. The so-called 'Global Gag Rule' was first introduced in 1984 and reintroduced by George W. Bush in 2001. It prohibits organisations in receipt of US funds from using their own money to provide abortion information, services and care, or even discussing abortion or criticising unsafe abortion.

Medical abortion
This type of abortion usually takes place after nine weeks of pregnancy. The same drugs are used as in early medical abortion, but the abortion takes longer and the pregnant woman may need a higher dose of the drugs.

Pro-choice
Pro-choice supporters believe that it is a woman's choice whether to have an abortion or not, as it is her body which is affected by the pregnancy. They believe the choice of abortion should be available to all.

Pro-life
Pro-life supporters believe that life begins at conception, and that the rights of an unborn child outweigh those of the pregnant woman. They believe the law should be changed so that abortion would be heavily restricted or outlawed in the UK.

Sanctity of life
A term used by religious believers (particularly Christians) to describe the sacred nature of all human life which has been created by God. It is often used in debates relating to abortion, euthanasia and cloning.

Surgical dilation and evacuation (D&E)
This type of abortion usually takes place after about 15 weeks of pregnancy. The cervix is dilated under a general anaesthetic and the pregnancy is removed in fragments using forceps and a suction tube.

Vacuum aspiration
Also called suction termination. This type of abortion usually takes place between seven and 15 weeks of pregnancy. A local anaesthetic is applied so that the cervix can be dilated and the contents of the womb removed using a small suction tube.

Viability
This refers to the capacity of a foetus to survive outside the womb. In UK law, the 24th week of pregnancy is the point at which the foetus is considered to be viable, and therefore the latest point at which an abortion can be performed: however, some people argue that this should be reduced as medical advances mean that some premature babies born at 24 weeks are surviving.

Zygote
Until day 14 of pregnancy, a fertilised egg is referred to as a zygote.

INDEX

ADDITIONAL RESOURCES

Other Issues titles

If you are interested in researching further the issues raised in *The Abortion Debate*, you may want to read the following titles in the **Issues** series as they contain additional relevant articles:

- Vol. 123 *Young People and Health* (ISBN 1 86168 362 6)
- Vol. 120 *The Human Rights Issues* (ISBN 1 86168 353 7)
- Vol. 102 *The Ethics of Euthanasia* (ISBN 1 86168 316 2)
- Vol. 96 *Preventing Sexual Diseases* (ISBN 1 86168 304 9)
- Vol. 94 *Religions and Beliefs in Britain* (ISBN 1 86168 302 2)
- Vol. 11 *Fertility Rights* (ISBN 1 86168 140 2)

For more information about these titles, visit our website at www.independence.co.uk/publicationslist

Useful organisations

You may find the websites of the following organisations useful for further research:

- British Medical Association: www.bma.org.uk
- British Pregnancy Advisory Service: www.bpas.org
- Brook Advisory Centres: www.brook.org.uk
- Department of Health: www.dh.gov.uk
- Education For Choice: www.efc.org.uk
- fpa: www.fpa.org.uk
- International Planned Parenthood Federation: www.ippf.org
- LIFE: www.lifeuk.org
- Marie Stopes International UK: www.mariestopes.org.uk
- National Youth Agency: www.youthinformation.com
- Pro-Choice Forum: www.prochoiceforum.org.uk
- RUThinking?: www.ruthinking.co.uk

ACKNOWLEDGEMENTS

The publisher is grateful for permission to reproduce the following material.

While every care has been taken to trace and acknowledge copyright, the publisher tenders its apology for any accidental infringement or where copyright has proved untraceable. The publisher would be pleased to come to a suitable arrangement in any such case with the rightful owner.

Chapter One: Abortion Facts

Religion, contraception and abortion, © fpa, *A humanist discussion of abortion*, © British Humanist Association, *Termination*, © National Youth Agency, *The legal position*, © British Pregnancy Advisory Service, *Coping with an unplanned pregnancy*, © iVillage UK, *Abortion and depression*, © Guardian Newspapers Ltd, *Dealing with an abortion*, © TheSite.org, *Abortion*, © fpa, *For men*, © Education For Choice, *Real life: abortion*, © RUThinking?, *Abortion statistics*, © Brook Advisory Centres, *Global Gag Rule*, © International Planned Parenthood Federation, *Unsafe abortion and poverty*, © World Health Organization.

Chapter Two: The Debate

Ethical consideration, © British Medical Association, *Abortion: the answer to unplanned pregnancy?*, ©

channel4.com, *The new pro-lifers*, © Guardian Newspapers Ltd, *Can a foetus feel pain?*, © University of Birmingham, *Foetal development*, © Education For Choice, *Viability*, © Education For Choice, *Abortion and confidentiality*, © Marie Stopes International UK, *Rights and wrongs of teenage abortion*, © Guardian Newspapers Ltd, *Teenage conceptions*, © Brook Advisory Centre, *DIY abortions*, © Associated Newspapers Ltd, *What's wrong with 'do-it-yourself' abortions?*, © Pro-Choice Forum, *UK aborts over 20 babies for minor disabilities*, © LIFE, *Abortion and disability*, © Pro-Choice Forum, *Women demand tougher laws to curb abortions*, © Guardian Newspapers Ltd, *The 24-week limit*, © Marie Stopes International UK, *Charity calls for Abortion Act review*, © LIFE, *YouGov abortion survey*, © YouGov.

Photographs and illustrations:

Pages 1, 15, 24: Simon Kneebone; pages 2, 17, 30, 35: Don Hatcher; pages 8, 19: Bev Aisbett; pages 9, 21, 34: Angelo Madrid.

Craig Donnellan
Cambridge
September, 2006